Morgan Le Fay's
BOOK OF SPELLS
AND WICCAN RITES

Morgan Le Fay's
Book of Spells and Wiccan Rites

Jennifer Reif

Citadel Press
Kensington Publishing Corp.
www.kensingtonbooks.com

CITADEL PRESS books are published by

Kensington Publishing Corp.
850 Third Avenue
New York, NY 10022

All Kensington titles, imprints, and distributed lines are available at special quantity discounts for bulk purchases for sales promotions, premiums, fund-raising, educational, or institutional use. Special book excerpts or customized printings can also be created to fit specific needs. For details, write or phone the office of the Kensington special sales manager: Kensington Publishing Corp., 850 Third Avenue, New York, NY 10022, attn: Special Sales Department, phone 1-800-221-2647.

Citadel Press and the Citadel logo are trademarks of Kensington Publishing Corp.

First printing June 2001

10 9 8 7 6 5 4 3

Printed in the United States of America

Cataloging data for this title may be obtained from the Library of Congress.

ISBN 0-8065-2200-3

Open your book of magic

Morgan Le Fay,

and reveal your secret arts.

O delver of the deep past, you have journeyed

across time, country, and memory, to learn your art.

Teacher, Priestess, Magician, Goddess. . . .

Come, reveal your wisdom to me.

Contents

Introduction: A History of Wicca

Wicca is an inspiring religious tradition colored by folklore, magic, and ancient myth. Unfortunately, its spiritual beliefs have often been misunderstood. The primary purpose of the following history is to help you to overcome any negative connotations you might associate with the words *Wicca* or *Witch*, and provide a broad base of understanding for the subject. The more our friends, coworkers, and family understand the history of Wiccacraft, the more accepting they will to be about its present-day resurgence.

The Wicca that is practiced today is for the most part an inheritance from the Celtic religion of the British Isles. Ireland, Wales, Northern Scotland, and Gaul (the coast of France) were strongholds of the Old Religion, and many of those who live there today retain old Celtic bloodlines.

The word *Wicca* is Old English and is derived from the Celtic word for willow. The branches of the willow tree are bendable and flexible, and its wood was, and is, used for baskets and other useful wickerwork. *Wiccar* came to mean wise, signifying flexibility and mental agility. *Wittan* meant *to see*, or *to know*. The word *Witch* has descended from the word *Wicca*.

Wicca seeks to link the votary with the divine by using myths that inspire hope, joy, and transcendent experience. The basic philosophy is that nature is sacred, its universal forces manifesting as Goddess and God. One important aspect of this spiritual view is that just as women give birth, the Goddess gives birth to all of life. Reflecting the myth of the Goddess and God are the Wiccan seasonal rites. These rites give divine attributes to the seasons, and bring us the awareness that we are each a part of the great river of life.

How did the word *Witch* get such negative connotations? It took centuries. We have to look at the influence of Roman Christianity upon Celtic religion in order to get a real understanding. But Wicca has deep roots that reach back thousands of years.

Twenty-five to thirty-five thousand years ago, the Paleolithic culture of central Europe included the worship of the Goddess. She was the ancestral Mother, the symbol of human and animal fertility and the powers of creation. The worship of the God began as the worship of the hunter and the hunted. He was the symbol of courage and of the powers of survival.

Two simple but important philosophies developed among the people of this period: animism and sympathetic magic. Animism ascribes spirits or deities to various aspects of nature. This is simply a way of seeing divinity in all living things, and to my mind an excellent idea. Sympathetic magic is the theory of like-attracts-like.

The advent of agriculture brought additional aspects to the Goddess and God. By 3000 B.C., the cultivation of grain had come to central Europe. The Goddess was now not only the ancestral Mother, but she was the land itself and the fertility of the crops. The God, who was the hunter and the death of the hunted, was eventually to become the harvested grain and therefore the death of the grain plant.

Many centuries later, a segment of the Indo-Europeans of central Europe became known as the Celts. A pantheon of gods and goddesses took central roles in their myths and rites. From this great reservoir of deities—mother goddesses, death goddesses, hero gods, and sacred lovers—came the deities who entered into the Wiccan holidays of Imbolc, Beltane, Lughnasad, and Samhain. Additional holidays for the solstices and equinoxes were also special points in the druids' (the Celtic priesthood) tree-month calendar. By the seventh century B.C., various clans and tribes of Celts had begun large-scale migrations throughout western Europe, taking their myths and holidays with them. Eventually they entered Britain.

Though today's Wiccan religion is primarily of Celtic origin, it has to some extent been influenced by Roman Paganism. In 55 A.D. Julius Caesar insisted that his armies cross the channel and move into Britain. There were several crossings, and after coming up hard against the Celts and the indigenous Picts, by 53 A.D. the troops had conquered land for Rome.

Roman Paganism remained the dominant religion in Rome, even in the first two centuries after the birth of Christ. At that point, Christianity appealed to the less powerful, to the non-aristocratic Romans. Mary was seen as the divine Mother, God the divine Father, and Christ the Savior-Son. While Christianity had begun as a religion for the downtrodden of both sexes, by the third century A.D. the doctrine of male leadership had become firmly established. Any variant tradition of Christianity was being challenged. Gnostic Christianity, which had been a mystical Christian tradition, was considered heresy.

In 324 A.D., the Roman Emperor Constantine officially converted from the Roman Pagan beliefs to Christianity, resulting in the union of church and state. The Roman aristocracy had no choice but to follow the example of their Emperor and convert. And so the Roman Empire merged with the Christian religion and Roman Catholicism began.

In 325 A.D., Emperor Constantine called a meeting of Roman Catholic high clerics. This was the Council of Nicaea where the trinity of Father, Son, and Holy Spirit was established. Abolished was the natural trinity of Father, Mother, and Son. Creed and theology were set down. Still, at this point Christianity was not yet the primary religion of the Roman people.

In 409 A.D. the Romans abandoned Britain and returned to the capital of the Empire; the Goths were sacking Rome. After four and a half centuries, the Romans no longer ruled Britain. They left their influences behind for Wicca to inherit and assimilate, their celebrations of the Fall and Spring Equinox. While the Roman grain goddess Ceres (fall), and the Maiden Flora (spring) did not enter the Celtic pantheon, their influences lingered.

By the end of the 5th century A.D., the Germanic peoples (the Saxons) were making a home for themselves in Britain and Gaul, bringing their influences into early Wicca. In particular their spring goddess Ostra had also worked her influence into the Spring Equinox themes.

Though the Roman government had left Britain and the power of the Roman Empire was waning, its church continued to grow. Time moved forward and the feudalism of the Middle Ages took over. At the same time, the church began to advocate celibacy for its clergy. Perhaps this was emblematic of Roman Catholicism moving ever farther away from nature.

The year 597 A.D. brought the Roman missionary Augustine to British soil. He began to convert Celtic Pagans to the Roman church. He presented Mary as a version of the Celtic goddess Brigid, and he compared Christ to the Celtic hero-god Cuchulain. Part of Augustine's mission was to bring the Briton-Celtic Christian church into the Roman church. The Celtic Christian church, primarily Britons and Roman descendants, had been developing independently of Rome. They gave women equal clerical status and used druidic poetic images of nature to reflect spirituality. Eventually the Celtic church was absorbed into the Roman church.

The ninth century brought Danish invasions to Britain, and by the tenth century there had been the Viking invasions. Celtic Paganism felt these influences. Coming as they did from so far north of the equator, and having so many dark days in their year, the effects of the sun were very important to the Scandinavians. Their invasions brought additional solar elements into Wicca, enriching the winter and summer solstice holidays.

The Roman church was sometimes challenged by its own clerics. In the twelfth century an Italian priest, Arnold of Bresica, felt that an excessive love of money and property, rather than true spirituality, had come to dominate the church. He tried to reform the church so that it would abandon its love of wealth and also eliminate the practice of confession of sins to a priest. He was exiled and his books burned. In the early thirteenth century, Francis of Assisi also felt that the church was lacking, but he was saved by his own eloquence. People liked Francis. He wrote about the divine beauty of nature, he had the magical power of drawing animals to him, and he was said to exhibit *stigmata*, bleeding wounds in the same places that Christ was wounded. Still, with all of his popularity, Francis came very close to being called a heretic. The church didn't like being challenged. This feeling about Francis that the church held foreshadowed the creation of the Inquisition. The Inquisition was basically a war against those who did not practice Roman Catholicism.

The question is, how on earth did a religious body justify creating a war? It is important to know that many of the Roman Popes, such as Innocent IV, were lawyers. The writing of law was part of their training and vocation. This extended to the writing of religious law, which was backed up by a church judicial system.

When several Popes wrote Papal Bulls against heretics, making it legal to prosecute Wiccans and Pagans, the Inquisition came one step closer to being manifested. (The phrase *Papal Bull* comes from the word *bulla*, which was a gold or silver seal used for authenticating documents.) In 1184, Pope Innocent III set up rules for arrest, inquiry, and punishment of heretics. In 1199 he added to this, creating law which equated heresy with treason. Because of this particular Papal Bull, heretics could be arrested for treason against God. This set the stage or the Inquisition.

In 1233, Pope Gregory IX established a permanent tribunal dedicated to stamping out heresy against the church. He called it the Inquisition. This infamous tribunal made use of legalized torture, imprisonment, confiscation of property, and the execution of heretics. The basic force created was one that was meant to frighten people away from non-Christian religions and accept Christianity as the only way of relating to divinity. In the mid-thirteenth century, Pope Innocent IV commissioned the first handbook of Inquisitorial procedure. In 1331, Inquisitor Bernardo Gui wrote another manual of procedure. In 1484 Pope Innocent VIII wrote a specific Papal Bull against Witches and Pagans.

In 1486 two monks, Heinrich Kramer and James Sprenger wrote what was to become an Inquisitor's guidebook called *The Malleus Maleficarum*. The title has been loosely translated as *The Witch Hammer*. Their book gave specific instructions on how to identify, prosecute, and punish Witches. Witches were called *Pagans*, which came to mean *Godless*. Christians adopted the use of the Latin word *Pagani*, which had at one time simply meant country dweller.

From the thirteenth through the eighteenth centuries, uncountable thousands of Wiccans were persecuted. The majority of those killed were women, though men frequently suffered as well. During the Inquisition, Wiccans were tortured into confessions and then burned at the stake in order to "save their souls." Once someone reported a relative, friend, or enemy to an officer of the Inquisition, the victim's property was taken and the negative outcome of the trial was almost a certainty. It took enormous courage for Wiccans to continue to practice their religion. At the same time, the rising male medical establishment used the Inquisition to stop village herbalists and midwives from practicing.

The asceticism of the Roman church began to disdain the physical world; there existed a destructive idea that saw spirit as good and flesh as bad. Priests beat themselves bloody with a scourge for having thoughts about sex, as well as other impieties, real or imaginary. Women were seen as either the good spiritual woman or as the evil temptress. Sadly, the Roman church brought a sense of shame to human sexuality.

Things took another unfortunate turn when the Roman church manufactured the idea and image of Satan. While negative influences in the world do exist, the *image* of Satan began as a propaganda image. Through the propaganda of the sermon, the church pieced together an image of an all-evil being using parts of various Pagan gods. They gave Satan the horns and hooves of the nature gods Cernunnos and Pan, and the trident of the Roman god Neptune. They gave him the fiery form of the Celtic Belenus, and the quadruple wings of the Babylonian cherubim.

To the church, Satan became the embodiment of anything that went against their laws and spiritual beliefs. One can observe that destruction becomes a part of human history every time a culture believes that their way is the "one true way" and then sets about subjugating others through force. When they do this, they become the very evil that they have spoken against.

The Roman church most probably took the name Satan from the Persian serpent god Shaytan. There is still a small sect in Iraq who worships Shaytan the serpent god. He is of the Jinn, or Djinn. While the Djinn began as ancestral spirits, over time they became like the Greek daemons, sort of troublemaking spirits. Shaytan's followers believe that their god governs the spirit world and must be placated by prayer in order to keep peace.

By making Satan the embodiment of all evil the church ended up creating what they most feared. Groups of people chose the image of Satan as a focus of worship. Their choice developed as a reaction to the harshness and rigid rules of the church as well as to the shame and powerlessness the church inspired.

Satanism has never been a part of Wiccacraft; it is a 180-degree turn from Christianity. Wicca remains a separate religion based in Celtic myth, a religion of country folk who were reminded of their Goddess and God at the change of the seasons, at the harnessing of the plow, and in the work and pleasure of the autumn harvest.

In 1604 King James passed a set of laws against Witchcraft, which did not differentiate between Wicca and Satanism. By 1611, he had put out his authorized version of the Bible, which is still in use today. It wasn't until over a century, later, in 1736, that the King James Witchcraft Act was repealed and replaced by a law that made it illegal to use occult powers.

By the eighteenth century the persecutions of the formal Inquisition had ended, but hideous stereotypes of Witches remained. After centuries of negative propaganda about Wiccacraft, its practitioners went underground. Pagan-Christians in the British Isles went to church during the day, but some still practiced the Old Religion at night. However, the idea of the "bad witch" doing "evil things" filtered into European fairy tales. From there the image became a part of mass consciousness, most children being fed ideas about all witches being bad and ugly through apparently innocent bedtime stories.

Now we come to the twentieth century. In 1921 Dr. Margaret Murray wrote *The Witch Cult in Western Europe*. The importance of this book was that for the first time, a scholar explained Witchcraft as a real religion. In 1931 she had another book published called *The God of the Witches*.

In 1951 England finally repealed the last of its Witchcraft laws. Perhaps this is what encouraged Gerald Gardner, a practicing British Witch, to have his book *Witchcraft Today* published in 1954. In it Gardner states that he was initiated into an English coven prior to the start of World War II. In 1959 another book followed titled, *The Meaning of Witchcraft*. The current tradition called Gardnerian Wicca has descended from him.

Then came Robert Graves's book *The White Goddess*. Published in 1959, it taught the world much about the Goddess. Included are the contributions of the Celts to Paganism, particularly important is Graves's translation of the Welsh "Battle of the Trees," in which he explains the druidic tree-months and gives references to the Celtic seasonal year.

Then we have a favorite of mine, that great personality, Witch and author Sybil Leek. She wrote many books about subjects from astrology to palmistry, but it was her books *Diary of a Witch* (1968) and *The Complete Art of Witchcraft* (1971) that really made waves. A vivacious and flamboyant woman, she charmed all with her wit and common sense. Descending from a long line of Witches, she sometimes appeared with her pet jackdaw (member of the raven family), Mr. Hotfoot Jackson.

Sybil Leek made it her work to explain to the world that Witchcraft was a sane, reasonable, bonafide religion, and she did this in style. Appearing on television, radio, and in the news, she presented Witchcraft as a way of living in harmony with nature. To bring attention to her cause she was photographed in San Francisco (among other events) raising the winds in 1967, and raising fire in a fireplace in the Hearst Castle in 1966. Her beliefs in the Divine Being, the Universal Mind, and the Creative Forces were made clear in her books.

Other important books followed: Raymond Buckland's *The Tree* (1974), about the tradition of Saxon Wicca, Merlin Stone's *When God Was a Woman* (1976), and Starhawk's *The Spiral Dance* (1979), from which the Reclaiming Tradition of Wicca has descended.

In 1981, Janet and Stuart Farrar's *Eight Sabbats for Witches* was published. The Farrars were trained by Alex and Maxine Sanders, and their own coven (a Gardnerian-Alexandrian tradition) began in 1970. Included in their rites are a High Priestess, High Priest, and the use of male-female partnerships for their magical work. Their excellent book includes passages from

Gerald Gardner's Book of Shadows, some of them written by Doreen Valiente.

Since the 1970s Wicca has flourished. It is an alternative religious choice which celebrates nature and our integral relationship to it. Like the current mainstream religions with their varying traditions, there are many different traditions of Wicca: Gardnerian, Alexandrian, Dianic, Fairie, Seax, and more. Today's evolving Wicca can combine elements of both western and eastern polytheistic traditions.

One important thing that all of the traditions have in common is a central belief in the Goddess as Creatress. So central is this belief that branches of today's Wicca (such as Dianic) do not include gods. Some traditions practice Goddess Religion and celebrate the Celtic holidays without using the words *Wicca* or *Witch* at all.

And so we come to this little book. I did not come from a hereditary line of Witches, nor was I trained in any specific school of modern-day Wicca. I learned from the books I have mentioned and others, and I am very thankful for those authors who have been my teachers. As the years have passed, I learned more about Wicca from within. The sacred images in Wicca have led me to honor nature and learn about the deities of many forms of Paganism from the world's ancient cultures.

The resurgence of Wicca is part of society's need to reconnect with the natural world. The celebrations of the eight Wiccan Sabbats connect us to nature's cycle of the seasons. The spells, prayers, and invocations work for us on a powerful personal level. Through Wicca we learn that nature is sacred, that miracles do indeed happen, and that transcendent experiences are not only for the sainted. The Wiccan religion deserves to take a place at the high table of the world's great faiths. It is not merely a guest, but has its own rightful seat among them all.

Morgan Le Fay's
Book of Spells and Wiccan Rites

Prologue

We all have challenges and desires that need to be met. In this book you will find rites and spells designed to draw you into the life-force and create a positive magical relationship with the forces in play. These forces live in the unconscious where dreams, passions, and a natural love for beauty revolve around our ideals and goals. Sacred life-forces appear to us as myths, archetypes, and deities that reside in the waters of the collective unconscious, which is a deep level of the psyche shared by all human beings. These universal images call out to us, ready to bring new awareness into our lives.

Each of us lives a story within which we are the principal character. As the heroine or hero of our own life, we can reach into the mythic structure of that life to create change and new experience. Positive thoughts and affirmations effect change, but when we add the power of ritual, the spark of magic is born.

Some people are afraid of the ideas of invocation and magic. As in everything, it is our intention that counts. What is an invocation but a form of prayer? And what is the outcome of magic but what some would call a miracle? The spells herein have been born from need. They are here to assist you. The more you focus your energies and commit your mind and heart to the rites, the more their power can enrich your life. May these spells and rites bring you blessings and help create the experiences and changes that you desire.

1

For Strength
and Power

To Athena, Warrior Goddess

For inner strength and power

This spell invokes the Greek goddess Athena. Candle-magic, visioning, and other magical actions allow you to take up her sword of strength. She will rise up within you and flow through you. Allow your focus to increase and build as you perform the rite each of the seven nights.

Items Needed   Goddess statue or vase of flowers; three white votive candles and holders; two yellow taper candles and holders; a wood-handled knife: scented oil of heliotrope, frankincense, or orange flower; a small dish of olive oil or olive leaves; and a cloth to wipe the fingers free of oil.

The Altar   Place the Goddess statue or a vase of flowers at the center back of your altar. Place the yellow taper candles to the right and left of this center piece. In front of these, in a horizontal line, place the three white votive candles. Place the knife horizontally in front of the votive candles. Set the olive oil on the altar. Place the cloth to the side of the altar; you may need it to wipe your hands after anointing with oil.

Timing and Instructions   The length of this rite is seven nights, to be done any time between the new and full moon. After the seventh night, place a portion of the offerings into the earth. Place the olive leaves or a little of the olive oil into the earth also.

Body of Ritual   Be seated at your altar. Take a deep breath and relax. Consider the strength and power that you seek. Begin by invoking her. Say:

> Athena, ancient Mother of Athens,
> Goddess of strength, courage, and power,
> Come, and attend this holy rite.

Light the two yellow taper candles and say: "For her strength and power." Then say:

> Great Warrior Goddess,
> With sea-blue eyes of piercing wisdom,
> And a heart of golden fire,
> The Sword of Victory stands ready at your side.
> To drums and flutes your dance begins.
> And as you dance, you let the power rise.
> The rhythms of your body enchanting me,
> Drawing me deeply into your power.
> Hail, Athena!

See Athena dance with sword and shield—magnificent, powerful, and beautiful to behold. Then say:

> Beloved Goddess,
> Before the shining light of your spirit,
> As in your deepening shadow,
> The enemies of freedom are vanquished
> And wisdom reigns.
> As you have come to women in their time of labor,
> And to armies in the heat of battle,
> As you have bestowed your great gifts upon
>   civilizations,
> So come to this one who calls out to you.

Light central white votive candle while saying "Hail, Athena!" Anoint the handle of the knife with the olive oil. Then say:

> Noble one,
> Within you lies the power

To stand strong before the adversary,
With a power and will never wavering.
And so I ask that you to bring
That strength and courage unto me,
As I open to the powers of the Warrior Queen.
Hail, Athena!

Close your eyes. Visualize her before you. See her approach you.
Open your eyes. See her in the flame. Say:

Your power is rising;
A strong breeze upon the Winds of Justice,
A calm knowing above the Sea of Wisdom,
I call forth my Warrior's Heart.

Breath her into your heart, and feel the power of the Warrior
Goddess. Then say *"Athena is with me."*
Then, stand and say:

Her power is rising.
I see as she sees.
I feel her power in my arms.
With ease, I hold the Sword of Strength
At my command are the Powers of Justice.
My legs shall carry me into battle as needs be.
I walk with pride into my destiny.

Feet apart, I stand strong and take my place in the
  world,
Expressing my own divinity.
I have the power to speak my mind with ease.
Or, if the battle requires,
In wisdom I may choose to keep my silence
And still my action
While my Warrior Heart remains alive and bright.
I hold the Sword of Strength.

Imagine that you hold her great sword. Feel its weight. Be seated and place the knife on your lap. Anoint the edge of the bowl of olive leaves or oil while saying:

> *You are with me, ancient queen,*
> *In the deepest recesses of my heart,*
> *Within my soul, my body, and my mind.*
> *O I am born, with the Warrior's Heart,*
> *For you, Athena, stand with me,*
> *Now and forevermore!*
> *So be it.*

Light the left votive candle while saying, *"I am born with the Warrior's Heart."*

Light the right votive candle while saying, *"Athena stands with me now and forevermore. And so it is."*

Close your fists, cross your arms over your chest, and bow your head. Back away from the altar. Later, after about fifteen minutes or so, extinguish the candles with a snuffer or inverted cup, saying for each candle, *"The flame is extinguished but the spell is unbroken."*

Perform this rite for six additional nights. On the last night, let the candles burn down completely.

THE HAND OF HECATE

For strength and success

In this spell you will invoke the Greek goddess Hecate and visualize her cavern, her cauldron, and her magic flame. Call upon her and ask for her blessings. She will attend you as you take on her divine attributes of strength, power, and success.

ITEMS NEEDED   A cauldron or image of a cauldron; a bowl of warm water; a mirror; bread and wine (or grape juice); one white or yellow votive candle and a votive holder; a candle snuffer or small cup; a censer; three censer coals, and incense made with 2 tablespoons ground myrrh, 1/2 teaspoon powdered ginger, and 4 tablespoons ground cedar (or a pre-made incense containing myrrh).

THE ALTAR   Set the cauldron or image of a cauldron and the mirror onto the altar. Place the mirror behind the cauldron but make sure you can still see it. Place the bowl of water inside the cauldron (or in front of your image of a cauldron). Have the bread and wine (or grape juice) beside the altar. Place the incense on the altar. Set the candle on the altar.

TIMING AND INSTRUCTIONS   Duration of this rite is three nights, to be done any time from the new moon to the full moon. After the rite, take several sips of wine (or juice), and eat a little bread. Place the remainder of the offerings outside on the earth.

BODY OF RITUAL   Light the censer coal. Be seated at your altar. Call out to Hecate, saying:

> *Hecate, holding torch and sickle,*
> *The sacred serpent entwined around your arm,*
> *You are the keeper of many paths to deep magic.*

> *O grandmother of the ancient cauldron,*
> *Come, hear my prayer.*

Set the offerings of bread and wine on the altar. State the matter in which Hecate's aid is needed. Pray to her. Then say:

> *Hecate, grant me your power*
> *That I may succeed in the matter at hand.*
> *Deep in your cavern,*
> *You spin the Web of Life,*
> *Connecting all things to each other*
> *As steam rises unhindered*
> *From the cauldron of the ages.*
> *May your wisdom and power rise to serve me.*

Sprinkle the incense on the coal. Raise the censer above, below, to the right, and to the left. Say:

> *Hecate,*
> *Mirrored in your cauldron are events past and*
>   *present,*
> *As you stir and enchant with magic,*
> *The turning future of mortal life.*
> *Wise One, I seek the blessings that are born*
> *From your mighty powers.*
> *O Goddess of the haunting moon and the silent*
>   *crossroads,*
> *Attend me!*

Light the candle, and say:

> *Grandmother of Holy Magic;*
> *Power of yellow running flame,*
> *Of dew under moonlight,*
> *Of all the blessed herbs,*

And of the star's ever-present powers,
I honor you.

Visualize the entrance to Hecate's cavern. When the image is firmly in your mind, say:

Into the depths of your cavern,
I stretch my hand, reaching to touch your
     incandescent powers.
Silver of stars, darkness of deep Earth,
I reach into the depths to touch the hand of Hecate,
And I find you.

Visualize Hecate in her cavern at her cauldron. She asks you to look inside the cauldron, where you see a sparkling liquid. She invites you to take from it. Dip your fingers into the bowl of water on the altar, imagining that you are dipping into the powers of Hecate's cauldron. Dampen your face, shoulders, arms, and hands with the water. Pass one hand quickly over the candle flame, then do the same with the other hand. Breathe in her power and her strength. Then say, and feel the following:

Saffron-Cloaked One,
Yellow and red flame rises into my soul,
The silver of your magic flows into my body,
And I am filled with your ancient power!

Look at your image in the mirror. Repeat the following lines one by one, looking into the mirror as you say each line.

I, ablaze with your Power,
Now reenter the path of my life.
You, Hecate, are with me, silent and powerful.
You are with me,
And strength is mine.

Your yellow and scarlet flame lives within my soul.
The power of the deep cavern is prepared.
Your silver magic flows through me.
I touch the hand of Hecate.

She is with me,
And success is mine.
She is with me,
And strength is mine.
Hail, Hecate!
So be it.

Sprinkle more incense on the lit coal in the censer. Extinguish the candle with a snuffer or an inverted cup, saying:

The flame is extinguished
But the spell is unbroken.

Repeat the rite for two additional nights. On the last night, let the candle burn down fully.

THE VESSEL OF ISIS

To awaken confidence and determination

In this spell you will invoke the Egyptian goddess Isis into your spirit. Herbs, scented oil, flowers, an image of Isis' wings, and your affirmations will be magically bound together within a vessel. The vessel will be sealed with the power of her name, and then opened and used the morning after the rite.

ITEMS NEEDED   A jar with a lid; one eight-inch circle of fabric with the name ISIS written on it; twine and scissors; a small image (sculpted, drawn, or copied) of outstretched wings; one red and three white votive candles in holders; a cinnamon stick, a censer; censer coal; frankincense; frankincense oil; one foot of red ribbon; a vase of blue flowers; and your list of affirmations (see TIMING AND INSTRUCTIONS, below).

THE ALTAR   Arrange the vase, the red candle, the censer, the frankincense oil, and the vessel on the altar. Keep the image of wings, the three white votive candles, and all other items ready on one side of the altar.

TIMING AND INSTRUCTIONS   Duration of this rite is one night, to be done any time between the new and full moon. Prepare for this rite by writing down affirmative statements regarding what you wish to achieve. After your statements write; "I, (your name) am prepared for change." Then write: "All things can change with the will of Isis."

BODY OF RITUAL   Place the frankincense on your lit coal. Read over your affirmations and then set them on the altar. Imagine a golden aura surrounding you and your altar. Imagine that you hear the flutter of wings. Feel that Isis is listening.

Light the red candle, and say:

> *Isis, you are the heart and throne of Egypt,*
> *Ruler and queen of the Two Lands.*
> *Mistress of magic and change,*
> *Lady of life, and of rebirth,*
> *Red and royal in your long, flowing robe.*
> *The holy uraeus crowns your head.*
> *Through you, Osiris lives again.*
> *Your wings beat above him;*
> *With words of power he lives again;*
> *For you are Isis.* *

Anoint a spot just above your heart with the frankincense oil, saying:

> *Come, O spirit of Isis,*
> *And descend unto this,*
> *The body of thy votary,*
> *And I shall weave magic,*
> *And create change.*

Take a deep breath, and imagine that you are drawing her into you. Say:

> *Here are the hands, the heart,*
> *And the soul of Isis.*

Place the frankincense on the coal. Pick up the vessel, invert it, and let fragrant smoke fill it. Say:

> *Here is the power of the sacred womb,*
> *The source and the soul of creation.*

*Most of this invocation was written by the author under the pseudonym Aila Daphne and first appeared in *The Isis Papers* no. 2, Los Angeles: Lyceum of Isis Pelagia, 1995, p. 5.

Pick up the image of the wings. Set it onto the altar, saying:

> *Wings . . . breath and magic of Isis,*
> *Live . . . in power.*

Anoint the rim of the empty vessel with the frankincense oil. Hold the vessel and say:

> *I am the shimmering heat of the desert,*
> *And the green banks of the Nile.*
> *Fragile blue flowers, by the river they rise.*
> *Gathered by gentle maidens in my name,*
> *Laid upon my golden altars,*
> *Deep blue flowers, their beauty sings my name;*
> *For I am Isis.*

Place three of the blue flowers into the vessel and say:

> *Here is the power of change and creation.*
> *For all things may change,*
> *As is the will of Isis.*

Pick up your affirmations and read them. Fold them up and place them into the vessel. Sprinkle more frankincense onto the coal in the censer. Say:

> *Libanum smokes from my holy altars,*
> *Where songs flow and magic is made.*
> *Timbrils and drums,*
> *Harps and flutes sing my praise.*
> *O I am the Holy Mother of the Two Lands,*
> *My body is sacred Egypt,*
> *Her river, her lands, her people,*
> *They remember me;*
> *For I am Isis.*

Place the wings into the vessel, saying:

> *Creature of mine,*
> *Flutter and raise the winds of change,*
> *Enter this vessel in magic,*
> *So that strength and determination*
> *Will grow even greater.*
> *Let it build . . .*
> *Growing into gentle waves of power.*

Place the cinnamon stick into the vessel, saying:

> *Perfect confidence and determination live.*
> *A light, born within this soul*
> *Grows greater and greater . . .*
> *Building into gentle waves of power.*
> *Through Isis shall the breath of power flow.*

Light one white candle and say, "*All things change with the will of Isis.*" Light the next white candle and say, "*Magic grows, and strength flows.*" Light the last white candle and say, "*The power has risen, for here is Isis!*"

Draw energy up from the Earth and down from the Heavens. Let the energy mix in your heart. Take a deep breath, and envision the word *Isis* many times within you. Pick up the vessel; take a breath and let the word *Isis* flow out as you exhale into the vessel. Repeat this several times. Seal the vessel with the lid, then place the circle of cloth over the top and tie the fabric around the neck of the vessel. Cense the vessel. Set the three white votive candles around it, and step away from your altar.

To release Isis, take a deep breath and exhale. Allow your body to bend forward as you exhale, and release all energies. Lie down and relax your body, allowing your mind to become empty and quiet. Let the vessel remain on the altar, and let the candles burn out completely.

On the morning following the rite, pour the contents of the vessel onto the cloth. Copy the affirmative statements onto another piece of paper and set this aside. Remove a one-inch piece of the cinnamon stick. Tie up the remaining contents into the cloth with the red ribbon and keep it as a charm.

Simmer the piece of the cinnamon stick with one and a half cups of water and a quarter teaspoon of orange zest for twenty minutes. Strain it into a cup and add honey. Read the affirmations as you drink the tea.

THE PENTAGRAM OF MORGAN LE FAY

For strength and wisdom

This spell invokes the Celtic magician-priestess Morgan Le Fay. In a visualization you will journey to her castle on the Isle of Avalon. She will teach you about the Pentagram of Strength and about special ancient letters called Ogham. The powers of these letters are used in the pentagram. From within, she will guide you to draw the pentagram, which will be hung on your wall after the ritual.

ITEMS NEEDED   A vase of white flowers; incense made from two tablespoons ground myrrh, five drops of rose oil, and four tablespoons ground pine or cedar (or just myrrh incense); a censer and censer coal; a bowl of salt and water; a seashell; three apples; a knife with which you will cut one of the apples; a small thorny rose branch; small green leafy branches; three white votive candles; three candle holders; an 8×10 inch square piece of white paper; a ten-inch piece of string, a pen and black ink; and a surface to write on.

THE ALTAR   Place the three candles in the center of the altar toward the front. Line them up in front of you, middle, left, and right. Keep the pen and paper to the side of the altar. Place the rest of the items on the altar.

TIMING AND INSTRUCTIONS   Duration of this rite is one night, to be done any time from the new moon to one day prior to the full moon. Keep in mind your specific goal or desire. You will be writing it on the reverse side of the pentagram.

BODY OF RITUAL   Light the censer coal ten minutes before the rite and then place a little incense on the coal. Cense the room that you will work in. Cense the altar. Pass the fragrant smoke carefully across your body, up to the top of your head and down to your feet. Put the censer down on the altar.

Light the center candle, and say:

> *Morgan Le Fay,*
> *Mysterious lady of green moors,*
> *Of the bright and shadowed moon,*
> *And of the misty sea,*
> *Arise from your vault of power,*
> *For I, your votary,*
> *Now come for your aid.*

Focus on the candle flame for a moment. Then say three times:

> *Lady of magic across the sea,*
> *Morgan Le Fay, I come to thee.*

Imagine that you are rowing a small boat across a sea. Then say:

> *I journey in an ash-hewn boat,*
> *Across the channel filled with mist,*
> *To find you upon the shores of the invisible isle.*
> *I ask that you, Morgan Le Fay*
> *Meet my soul beyond the heavenly sea,*
> *In that place called Avalon.*

Visualize the Blessed Isle out ahead of you. Then say:

> *Time stands still.*
> *Behind me lies the past,*
> *While before me lies your sacred domain.*
> *The mist begins to part;*

*A clear light breaks to reveal your isle of rest and
     renewal.
Green hills rise beyond the shore,
Beyond the golden sands of Avalon.
Here is your castle of Glamorgan.
Surrounded with briar and apple trees.*

*Upon Avalon you dwell in magic and beauty,
Bringing the light of courage unto Glamorgan's halls.
There, unwavering strength and wisdom live,
And heroic deeds of the future await their time.*

Light the candle to the right saying:

*Morgan Le Fay,
I call upon your ancient power.
Come, guide me.
Bring me strength and wisdom,
As you teach me the ways of your holy pentagram.*

Light the candle to the left, saying, *"Teach me."*

Visualize pulling your boat up on the beach. Turn and see
Morgan Le Fay walking toward you, down the hillside to the
shore. She wears long, flowing garments and carries a walking
stick. You hear the waves lapping upon the sand. Soon she faces
you. Her eyes have an inner light, and their glow penetrates
your soul. She speaks your name, telling you to watch her.
Using the point of her walking stick, she begins to draw something on the wet sand. Then, silently, mysteriously, she draws
you into her body until *you* are the one drawing on the wet
sand. Feel yourself drawing a circle in the wet sand with your
walking stick.

The Pentagram

Reach for the pen and paper near your altar. As she draws in the sand, you will draw on the paper. Draw a large circle on your paper. On the reverse of the sheet, write a phrase or sentence that embodies what it is you need her strength and wisdom for. Turn the paper over so that the circle is visible. Then, as if you are speaking as Morgan Le Fay, say:

> *I call upon the powers of the Morrigan*
> *For whom I was named,*
> *Upon the black raven who moves beyond time.*
> *Wild creature of wisdom and magic,*
> *I ask that Your powers enter this pentagram.*

Write the word *Morrigan* just above the outside of the circle at the top (see Figure 1). Then say:

> *I call upon Danu, our Mother of Earth,*
> *For we are all her children.*
> *It will be she, upon whom we write our future.*
> *Green hills, golden sands, deep Earth;*
> *Danu, I ask that your powers enter this pentagram.*

Write the word *Danu* just outside the lower-right portion of the circle (see Figure 1). Then say:

> *I call upon Ogma, shining scholar*
> *Who has brought us the marks of the ogham.*
> *These are the signs that we will use*
> *To carry our magic from thought to form.*
> *O powers of the ogham, enter this pentagram.*

Write the word *Ogma* just outside the lower-left portion of the circle (see Figure 1). Now, repeat writing the word *Ogma*

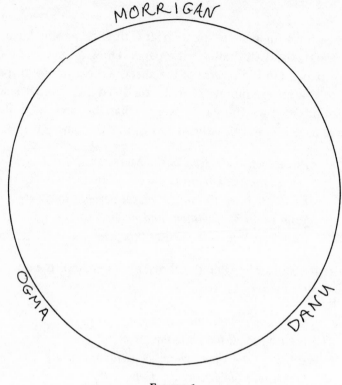

FIGURE 1

around the edge of the circle until you come to the word *Danu*. From the word *Danu*, repeat writing the word *Danu* around the edge of the circle until you come to the word *Morrigan*. Then from the word *Morrigan* repeat writing the word *Morrigan* around the rest of the edge of the circle (see Figure 2 for this).

Pick up one of the apples. Cut it in half widthwise. This will reveal the pentagram inside. Place the two halves on the altar with cut sides facing you. Say:

> *From the fruited tree that grows from Danu's body,*
> *Five points create the star of bliss.*

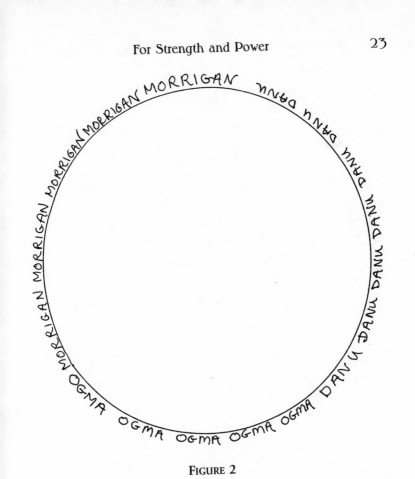

FIGURE 2

Draw a five-pointed star inside the circle, its points touching the inner edge of the circle. Draw it point up (see Figure 3).

Top Star Point

Prepare to write your first ogham, *Ailim*, in the top point. Say:

> *Ailim, power of the silver fir tree*
> *Growing high on the mountainside . . .*
> *Grant me clear vision and perception*
> *As I focus on the goal at hand,*

FIGURE 3

Seeing it in truth and clarity.
O power of the Silver Fir,
Enter into this pentagram
As I write the ogham for Ailim.

Now draw the ogham for Ailim in the top point of the star. Draw a vertical line and near the line's center point, draw one horizontal to cross it. Below this ogham write the word *Ailim*. In the center space of the pentacle below the top point of the star, write the words *Silver Fir* (see Figure 4).

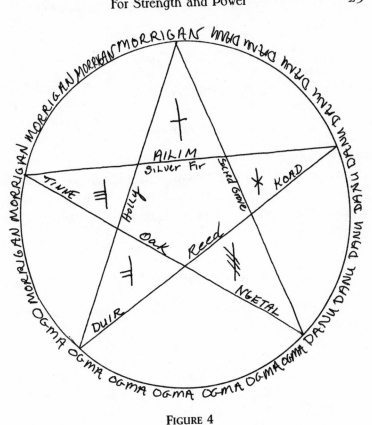

FIGURE 4

Upper-Right Star Point

Prepare to write your next ogham, *Koad*, in the upper-right point. First say:

> *Koad, the power of the sacred grove,*
> *All wisdom and knowledge arise from thee . . .*
> *Past, present, and future.*
> *Embraced by your circle of trees,*
> *I receive guidance from the divine.*

> *Roots deep, branches to the heavens,*
> *Connector of Earth and Sky,*
> *You bring me the unending circle of knowledge.*
> *O power of the Sacred Grove,*
> *Enter into this pentagram*
> *As I write the ogham for Koad.*

In the upper-right point of the star, draw the ogham for Koad: Draw one vertical line with two diagonal lines crossing it like an X. Next to the ogham write the word *Koad*. In the center space of the pentacle, below the upper-right point of the star, write the words *Sacred Grove* (see Figure 4).

Lower-Right Star Point

Prepare to write your next ogham, Ngetal, in the lower-right star point. First say:

> *Ngetal, power of the reed*
> *Growing at the river bank . . .*
> *You are like the arrow, tall and straight,*
> *Ready to fly to its mark.*
> *Through you I know my direction, even in chaos.*
> *Through you I am prepared for action, in power and*
>   *surety.*
> *I shall fly to my goal as the arrow flies to its mark.*
> *O power of the reed,*
> *Enter into this pentagram*
> *As I write the ogham for Ngetal.*

Now draw the ogham for Ngetal: In the lower-right point of the star, draw one vertical line. Draw three lines crossing it at an angle, each crossing line higher on the left and lower on the right. Below the ogham write the word *Ngetal*. In the center space of the pentacle below the lower-right point of the star, write the word *Reed* (see Figure 4).

Lower-Left Star Point

Prepare to write your next ogham, Duir, in the lower-left point. First say:

> *Duir, power of the ancient oak . . .*
> *Royal tree of bards and Druids,*
> *Tree of long life, and of enduring strength,*
> *I summon your powers.*
> *You endure through fire and lightning*
> *To emerge anew with leaves of green.*
>
> *Steady and sure, you are the strength of the world,*
> *Just as you are the door*
> *The spiritual gateway to realms beyond.*
> *O power of the ancient oak,*
> *Enter into this pentagram.*
> *As I write the ogham for Duir.*

Now draw the ogham for Duir: In the lower-left star point draw one vertical line. Near the middle of this line, draw two horizontal lines that extend out to the left. Below the ogham write the word *Duir*. In the center space of the pentacle below lower-left point of the star, write the word *Oak* (see Figure 4).

Upper-Left Star Point

Prepare to write your next ogham, Tinne, in the upper-left point. First say:

> *Tinne, power of the green holly . . .*
> *Tough and spiny in winter,*

From you shall hungry animals keep away.
Evergreen throughout the year,
You sustain your strength through all seasons.
With you I shall be safe and victorious.
O power of the green holly,
Enter into this pentagram,
As I write the ogham for Tinne.

Now draw the ogham for Tinne: In the upper-left star point, draw a vertical line and from it draw three even horizontal lines out to the left, like a reversed letter E. Below the ogham, write the word *Tinne*. In the center space of the pentacle below the upper-left point of the star, write the word *Holly* (see Figure 4).

Completing the Pentagram

Next, draw a small circle in the center of the pentacle. Draw a small five-pointed star inside the circle, point up. Add any decoration you want to the pentagram, spirals, moons, stars, and so on (see Figure 5). Hold the pentagram to your heart and say:

Power of Ailim . . . the silver fir,
Grant me clear vision.
Power of Koad . . . the sacred grove,
Bring me spiritual wisdom.
Power of Ngetal . . . the reed,
Guide me with perfect direction.
Power of Duir . . . the oak,
With you my strength endures.
Power of Tinne . . . the green holly,
Bring me victory!

FIGURE 5

Press the pentagram to your heart. Feel its power flood you; then roll it into a scroll and tie it with the piece of string. For the moment, place it under your shirt or blouse.

Visualize yourself again upon Avalon's shore. See the pentagram on the sand and the walking stick in your hand. Look up and see Morgan Le Fay's approval. Place the walking stick back in her hand and thank her for her gift. She bids you farewell, and returns to Glamorgan. Release her from your need. Board your boat and travel away from the blessed isle to return to where you live.

When you are ready, remove the pentagram from its holding place. Place it on the altar several inches in front of the candles and say:

> Many thanks to the Morrigan,
> To Danu and Ogma.
> May the signs of the ogham continue to teach me,
> As the powers of Morgan Le Fay's pentagram
> Enter into my life.
> So be it.

Unroll the scroll and tape the pentagram to the wall of your bedroom. Extinguish the candles, saying, "*The candles are extinguished, but the spell is unbroken.*"

The Morning After the Rite

Relight the candles and meditate on the ogham while you consider your situation. See yourself achieving your goal in strength and wisdom. Let the candles burn down completely. You may want to frame your pentagram, or prepare it in some way so that you can place it on a wall in the room in which you sleep. You may want to color it, or, you can roll it up and keep it in a special place.

2

For Healing
and Protection

THE BLESSINGS OF HYGEA

To gain health and vitality

In this spell you will invoke Hygea, the Greek Goddess of Health, daughter of Asclepius, the Healing God (see also "In the Temple of Asclepius"). With this rite, you will enter Hygea's garden and she will attend you, ministering to you in her perfect way. In a visualization you will drink the healing elixir that she offers, and image ill-health dropping away. You will receive guidance and healing, as you remain under her loving care.

ITEMS NEEDED A glass, cup, or chalice containing four ounces of distilled water; sandalwood stick incense; an incense holder; a vase of greenery and flowers; three green taper candles (one for each night of the ritual) in a holder; and small green leafy branches to surround the chalice.

THE ALTAR Set the candle in the center of the altar. Arrange the other items on the altar as you choose. Arrange the green branches around the chalice of water.

TIMING AND INSTRUCTIONS The duration of this rite is three nights, any time between the new moon to the full moon. Before the rite, take a bath in which you have placed two handfuls of Epsom salts. Wear something loose and comfortable during the rite.

BODY OF RITUAL Make sure there is plenty of ventilation in the room. Cense the room and the altar with the sandalwood incense. Cense around your body three times by passing the stick behind and in front of you, hand to hand. Extinguish stick and set it aside on altar. Sit before the altar and call out to Hygea:

> *Hail, Hygea!*
> *Holy daughter of the goddess Rhea.*
> *Crowned the Great Healer of your people,*
> *Your generous compassion is given to ailing humanity.*
> *To you who are wise in the ways of healing,*
> *I pray, and commend myself to your power.*

Light the green candle and say:

> *You have called me to your sacred garden.*
> *The candle burns, and your garden appears.*
> *The candle burns, and healing begins to take place.*

> *I come to you, Blessed Lady,*
> *And wait amid the lush green of tall grasses.*
> *Here sweet flowers grow in profusion:*
> *Roses and larkspur,*
> *Poppies, and hyacinth, and sweet meandering violets.*
> *Cool and clean is the air of this place.*
> *I am prepared for you,*
> *And am ready to be renewed.*
> *Come Lady, and bless me with your powers!*

Visualize her approaching you in the garden, in all her beauty and power. Taking as much time as you need, allow her to touch or embrace you in some healing way.

See her bless a special healing drink, making it a healing elixir. She asks you to pick it up. As you do, envision your glass or chalice of water swirling with gold and silver light. Pick up the glass on the altar and hear her say:

> *I have brought a healing draught*
> *To bring change into your body,*

To course through your veins,
To cleanse and purify you.
Come, beloved, and drink.

Again, see the liquid in the cup swirling with gold and silver light. Lift it to your lips and imagine that you are drinking her powers, her magic, and then say:

I am flushed with the powers of this elixir.
I breathe freely.
My face is warm and rosy with life.
My whole body comes into balance.
It hums, and renewal begins.

Relight the incense. Cense your body three times, by passing the incense stick around you from hand to hand, as well as from head to foot. Say:

The old shell that was my ill health drops away.
I easily let it go.
I step out from it,
To become bright and reborn.
Hygea is within me,
Guiding me to all that I need.
Guiding me, so that healing can take place.
Praises and thanksgiving to Hygea,
For her blessings and loving care.
So it is, and shall be.

Pause for a moment in stillness and quiet. Repeat the ritual for two additional nights, letting the candle burn down completely each night.

(Remember, for any illness, seek professional medical advice. This rite is intended as an aid to any medical care, not as a substitute for it.)

THE GEM WEB

A visualization for protection

This visualization will give you a sense of safety and comfort. With divine blessings, you will wrap yourself in an airy cocoon of sacred protective light.

ITEMS NEEDED   A comfortable place to lie down.

THE ALTAR   Your imagination.

TIMING AND INSTRUCTIONS   This rite can be done any time of the month. Read through the visualization at least once before you begin. Choose the place where you will lie down. You will be visualizing colored gems around you: a green gem above your head, a red gem at your feet, a blue gem at your right, and a yellow-gold gem at your left. Strands of light will pass through the gems and over and around your body. An optional way of performing this rite is to tape-record it, and then lie down and listen to the recording as you visualize each step.

BODY OF RITUAL   (In the second stanza below, you may wish to replace the phrase "Great Mother" with the name of a favored deity.) Before you lie down, say:

> *Red to blue,*
> *Green to gold,*
> *Light encircle body and soul.*
> *Web of power in harmony*
> *Bring perfect protection unto me,*
> *And so . . . it . . . shall . . . be!*

Lie down and begin to focus your mind upon your third eye (in the center of your forehead). Say:

Great Mother,
Bless my mind, my heart,
And my visioning powers.

Visualize a violet light emanating from the center of your fore-head, glowing and expansive. See a slight silvery quality to the light. Visualize it becoming more and more silver, until it becomes silvery white. Expand this light so it covers your entire body and extends about a foot around you—above your head, below your feet, everywhere. Float in it. Feel its strengthening and enlivening energies.

Just above your head, envision a green gem; see it bright and sparkling. Then, below your feet, see a red gem; see it also as bright and sparkling. Let lines of light flow across the front of your body from the red gem above your head to the green gem at your feet. Let the lines circle your body from top to bottom with strands of light. See the lines of light pass through the gems as they circle. Repeat this movement of light several times.

Next, to the right of your body see a deep-blue gem; see it bright and sparkling. Then, to the left of your body, see a yellow-gold gem; see it bright and sparkling. Let lines of light flow over you from the blue gem at your right to the yellow gem at your left, circling your body from side to side. The lines of light pass through the gems as they circle. Repeat this move-ment of light several times.

Now circle strands of light clockwise around your body, from the top of your head to your right side, to your feet, left side, and back up again: green, blue, red, and yellow. Let the strands of light pass through the gems as they circle you. Do this several times.

Next let lines of light intersect and cross over you, many times, until you are in a soft, flexible web of iridescent, glowing light. Feel this happening on all sides of your body: front, back, right, and left. When this is done, say:

Red to blue,
Green to gold,
Light encircle body and soul.
Web of power in harmony.
Brings perfect protection unto me,
And so . . . it . . . shall . . . be!

To Holy Sophia

To bring peace and calm

In this rite you will call out to Sophia, the wise and compassionate Gnostic Mother Goddess. Full of miracles, she is one who heals the sorrowing heart. As you visualize her, she will come and bring you all you need.

ITEMS NEEDED   Three candles: one yellow, one white, and one purple or lavender; myrrh or frankincense stick incense and holder; and a small bowl of water.

THE ALTAR   Arrange candles in a semicircle with the open end facing you. Place the small bowl of water in front of the candles. Place incense in the holder on the altar.

TIMING AND INSTRUCTIONS   The duration of this rite is one night and can be done during any lunar phase and may be repeated as desired. Make sure you have proper ventilation for the incense.

BODY OF RITUAL   Light the incense and cense the altar. Then put out the incense for the time being. Return to the altar and say:

> *Holy Sophia!*
> *From the door of your heavenly house,*
> *You let flow your thousand rays of illumination,*
> *And even the most stubborn of shadows*
> *Are dispelled with speed.*
>
> *Above your sacred portal,*
> *Rest the purest of white doves*
> *And the curling leafy vines of the grape,*
> *Heavy with sweet fruit.*

> *Sophia, standing at this gate between the worlds,*
> *You await the call of those who need you.*
> *All-Knowing Mother,*
> *The wisdom of the worlds is thine.*
> *Pearl of the Sacred Marriage between heart and soul,*
> *Between this world and the one beyond,*
> *You await your children's call.*
> *Lady, I who am now in need, call to you.*
> *Come to me!*

Envision Holy Sophia standing below her portal of white doves, then say:

> *Blessed One,*
> *The world has torn my heart,*
> *Like a raging tempest that fights itself*
> *Upon a dark sea of tears.*
> *I ask that you return to me my joyful heart.*
> *Make peace for me between the world within,*
> *And the world without.*
>
> *Wise and compassionate Mother,*
> *Create your miracle*
> *And send your holy doves into my soul.*
> *Let the flutter of their soft white wings*
> *Soothe my sorrowing heart.*
> *Release from me all that is foreign,*
> *And not of my own pure and holy spirit.*

Envision a soft breeze made by the flutter of wings. Feel the edges of dove wings gently touch your body. See Sophia touch you with purifying waters. Dip your fingers into the water and run them over your face. Dip the fingers in water again, and run them over your arms, legs, and whole body, allowing the water to cleanse any negative energies from you. Say:

Sophia,
Purified, I open to your light.
Breath of light, flutter of wings,
Pure and shining one,
You stand in the doorway of my soul,
The smiling sweet countenance of peace.
Enter here and reign in harmony.

Light the yellow candle and say, *"Your light shines into the deepest recesses of my soul."*

Light the white candle and say, *"Your holy doves bring peace into my heart."*

Light the purple or lavender candle and say, *"Your wisdom calms my soul."* Then say:

Beloved Mother,
Stay with me, illuminating my life with your powers.
Grant my prayer, that I may remain a soul in peace.
Grant me the wisdom to remain so,
As I honor you, saying,
Hail, Sophia!

Bow your head and let the candles burn down completely.

PRAYER TO THE BLACK MADONNA

To heal pain

In this candle-lighting prayer, the Black Madonna will come to your aid. She understands the darkness and pain of your sorrow, and so can heal you with her loving understanding. Honor her, pray to her, and receive her blessings.

ITEMS NEEDED   Five purple or lavender candles in holders; frankincense, myrrh, censer coal, and a censer; a vase of flowers of mixed colors; a bowl of white flower petals; and an image of the black Madonna, either a statue or a votive picture, or any image of Mary surrounded by black stones or black beads.

THE ALTAR   Arrange the five candles in a semicircle, with the open side toward you. Place the Madonna image in the center, facing you. Place the rest of the items on the altar.

TIMING AND INSTRUCTIONS   The duration of this rite is one night and can be done at any time during the lunar cycle. Light the censer coal five minutes ahead of the rite, and make sure that there is proper ventilation in the room.

BODY OF RITUAL   Be seated at your altar. Place the frankincense and myrrh on the censer coal. Light the first candle on the left side of the semicircle and say:

> *O Holy Mother,*
> *Serene in your dark beauty,*
> *You who have known both sadness and tears,*
> *Yet have known the joy beyond all tears,*
> *Hear me now.*

Light the second candle and say:

> *Santa Madre, Blessed Mother,*
> *I know that your power is great,*
> *That wondrous miracles have occurred in your name,*
> *And so I ask you now for your divine intervention.*
> *O come to my aid!*

Light the third candle and say:

> *Mother of gentle compassion,*
> *You know my dreams and my sorrows,*
> *And so I place the difficulties I have suffered*
> *Into your blessed hands.*

Light the fourth candle and say:

> *Mother of mercy,*
> *Of beauty and grace,*
> *Bless and heal my soul and my life.*

Light the fifth candle and say:

> *I pray to you in joy, loving Mother,*
> *For I know*
> *That you will transform me and heal me,*
> *With your dark and mysterious powers.*
> *Hail, Mary!*
> *So be it.*

Scatter white flower petals around her image. Pray to her as you will. Open to receive her blessings. Let the candles burn down completely.

IN THE TEMPLE OF ASCLEPIUS

To bring healing dreams

In ancient Greece, those seeking aid from the God of Healing went to his temple in Epidaurus. There they spent the night in the sanctity of his temple. In the morning they would awake healed or having had a dream of instruction to assist in healing. The walls of the temple were covered with votive objects and plaques commemorating healings of appreciative recipients of the God's blessings. In the rite, you will create his temple and call him to your aid. He will assist you with kindness and caring, as you perform the rite within the ancient temple.

ITEMS NEEDED   Four votive candles in holders set on plates; myrrh resin and incense coal (or myrrh stick incense); censer; four pieces of paper of approximately 8 × 10 inches; a brown felt marker and a surface upon which to write; four glasses of water each holding a white carnation and greenery; a pen and notebook; and a bowl containing fresh white carnation petals, dried mugwort, and dried thyme.

THE ALTAR   Use four small tables or other surface as altars, one on each side of the room in which you will sleep, with a votive candle placed upon each. (Use a table or other safe surface rather than the floor. Do not place the candle too close to the wall or any other object. Votive candles in votive holders are the best for the purpose.) Place a glass containing the white carnation and greenery next to each candle. Place the censer, incense, bowl of flower petals and herbs, and the writing utensils on the east altar.

TIMING AND INSTRUCTIONS   Duration of the rite is one night and can take place at any time of the lunar cycle. There will be activities the day after the rite. Decide on an offering of public service or volunteer work prior to the rite. The offering to Asclepius will be done on the day following your rite. Place the pen and notebook near your bed. The morning after the rite, you will write down your dreams before you get up.

BODY OF RITUAL   Be seated on a chair in the center of your bedroom. Begin, saying:

> Asclepius,
> Kind and gentle God of Epidaurus,
> Lord of the healing arts,
> One hand upon the caduceus
> And the other held out to us all,
> You offer healing and remedy through the power of
>   dreams.
> Through many centuries,
> Your votaries came to pray for your guidance.
> They slept within your heavenly temple
> Where they obtained cures, answers, and visions
> Through nights spent with the Healing God.
>
> Therefore, shall I spend the night in your holy temple,
> In the comfort of your divine protection.
> Your priests shall minister unto me.
> Here will appear your ancient temple,
> And I, safe within its walls,
> Will hear your words.
> I will learn the knowledge that you have for me.
>
> Whether it shall be herbs and medicines,
> Or foods added or abstained from,
> Whether it shall be massage to an ailing body,
> Or words of power, or potent healing thoughts.
> There may be some deed or action to be performed,

A letter that must be written,
Or special healers to find,
Or prayers that need to be spoken.

Whatever the remedy, you shall guide me
For your powers are those of the greatest good,
And in your compassion
You aid those who are suffering.
O powerful Asclepius, enter into the place.
My offering to you is a promise of service to others.

Using the marker, write his name on a piece of paper using Greek letters: ΑΣΚΛΕΠΙΟΣ. Place it upon the north altar and light the candle on that altar below his name, saying, *"Here is the northern wall of the Temple of Asclepius."*

Write his name again on another piece of paper: ΑΣΚΛΕ–ΠΙΟΣ. Place the paper on the east altar and light a candle, saying, *"Here is the eastern wall of the Temple of Asclepius."*

Write his name a third time: ΑΣΚΛΕΠΙΟΣ. Place the paper on the southern altar and light a candle, saying, *"Here is the southern wall of the Temple of Asclepius."*

Finally, write his name a fourth time: ΑΣΚΛΕΠΙΟΣ. Place the paper on the western altar and light a candle, saying, *"Here is the western wall of the Temple of Asclepius."*

Light the myrrh incense and cense the walls and ceiling, saying, *"Blessings upon the Temple of the God."*

Pick up the bowl of flower petals and dried herbs. Stand in the center of the room and draw white-light energy up from the Earth through your feet. Draw blue-light energy down from the heavens through the top of your head. Watch the energies swirl and mix in your heart area. Send the energy out through your arms, directing it through your hands to the bowl of flower petals and herbs. Visualize the bowl as full of light. In a clockwise direction from north, to east, to south, to west, sprinkle the contents of the bowl onto the plate under each candle on each altar as you say, *"The power of Asclepius shall attend me."*

Set the bowl down near the candle on the eastern altar. Make sure you have your notebook and pen ready for use in the morning, and prepare for bed. Lie down and breathe in and exhale, release and relax. Let yourself sink into the bed, becoming more and more relaxed. Know that you sleep within the temple of the healing god. Feel his kindness and caring reach out to you. You are safe within his care . . . Good night. . . .

When you awake, write down your dreams; everything you remember about them. Also write any thoughts, feelings, or ideas that come to you.

That day, do the service that you have planned as an offering to the God. Pass out sandwiches to the homeless, give a donation, clean up a local beach or park, and so on. That evening, review your notes. Look for direct healing advice, and also for a psychological pattern or idea that reveals what you need. Work with your dreams, and write out your interpretations of their messages. Find the patterns and messages of guidance. Create positive actions or change in your life based on these. Give your thanks and praises to Asclepius.

(Remember, always seek professional medical advice for illness; this rite is intended as a supplement to medical treatment.)

THE MOTHER'S BLESSINGS

A prayer to bring health

This is a simple but powerful spell.

ITEMS NEEDED   A Goddess statue, picture, or icon; one taper candle in a holder; and a vase of white flowers.

THE ALTAR   Arrange the above items on your altar.

TIMING AND INSTRUCTIONS   At dawn.

BODY OF RITUAL   Be seated at your altar. Light the candle and say:

> *Great Mother,*
> *Come, and grant me your blessings.*
> *Heal me and fill me with peace.*
> *As the sun rises, I listen for your holy words.*
> *Come, set them upon the altar of my heart.*

Visualize the Great Goddess attending you. She speaks to you. Feel her words:

> *May showering beams of heavenly light*
> *Descend upon you and fill you with peace.*
> *Beloved one, may your heart be filled with joy*
> *As your body comes into harmony.*
> *Your mind and body come into balance; Therefore are*
> *   you comfortable and strong.*
> *Your body renews, repairs, and heals itself with divine*
> *   powers.*
>
> *Time moves forward, and you find all that you need*
> *To bring you into a state of good health.*

You are guided to right actions, which serve your
  sacred body
And keep it whole and sound.

Blessed by the light of ever-flowing Spirit,
And the beauty of the Everlasting,
Health is yours to honor and enjoy.
The Mother's blessings are upon you,
And so it is, and shall be.

Place your hands over the candle flame. Imagine that you take
up the energy of the flame with your hands and cover your
body with it. Do this several times, until your body is bathed in
the flame's energy. When you are done, go outside and watch
the sunrise. Let the candle burn down completely. Visualize that
you draw in the rays of the morning sun.

THE GIFT OF DIANA

Letting go of past sorrow

When you still feel sorrow due to past experiences with others and have done all you can in the way of communication and action with that person or persons, then come to Diana. Hers is a magic that can heal and mend deep memory. Work with her and bring balance into your heart. She can bring healing where you may have thought it would never be possible. This rite requires a commitment to go deeply within, to see and feel, and with her aid, to let go.

ITEMS NEEDED   White flowers in a vase; seven white candles in holders; a knife; a metal or heavy ceramic bowl; tongs; a spade; a handful of Epsom salts; pen and paper; incense made of two parts pounded myrrh resin, a half-part powdered cinnamon, and one part dried crushed mint; a censer and censer coal.

THE ALTAR   Arrange the flowers, candles, and censer on the altar, with the seven candles in a "half diamond" pattern, before you. The point of the half diamond should be toward the back of the altar while the open end faces you. Place the pen, paper, knife, bowl, and tongs to the side of the altar.

TIMING AND INSTRUCTIONS   The duration of the rite is one night. It is to be done while the moon is waning, and there is one follow-up morning activity. The rite is to be performed only after you have done everything to facilitate action, communication, and honest relationships with others. If you feel that there is nothing more you can do in the outside world, then it is time for you to do the inner work. In the candle-lighting section you need to participate in and respond to the Goddess's commands, participating in the inner work that is required. This is an in-depth process that is between the Goddess and you. Be patient with your part of the process.

BODY OF RITUAL   Place a little incense on a lit censer coal. Wait for the smoke to rise, then say:

> *Lady, many have been my sorrows;*
> *Innocent gifts of love,*
> *And gardens of paradise,*
> *Battered and crushed at other's hands.*
>
> *A hand held out in trust,*
> *The shattered illusion of perfect human love,*
> *These are the dark pools of memory*
> *About which I pray.*
> *Diana, wise Mother of all things,*
> *Come and heal my soul.*

Sprinkle more incense on the coal, then say:

> *I have done what I can,*
> *To write, to talk, to speak the truth.*
> *I have done what I can,*
> *To banish the pain from my mind.*
> *But I am still injured*
> *And the pain still rises in my memory.*
> *I am in need of one more powerful than I,*
> *And so I pray, Diana, come and heal my soul.*

Sprinkle more incense on the coal, then say:

> *O Queen of Earth and Heaven,*
> *Mistress of hope and courage,*
> *Lady of magic that heals and mends,*
> *Hear my prayer.*
> *Help me to release these past sorrows.*

It is my desire to give up my burden.
And so I pray, Diana, come and heal my soul.

Sprinkle more incense on the coal, then say:

Lady, even in shadow does hope ascend.
For you now stand before me.
Your prism-colored light seeps into my soul
As you urge me to step out from my aging armor.
Speak to me, O Lady who is Goddess of all things.

Hear her words, allow them to enter your heart as she speaks:

"I, Diana, carry within my divinity,
The scales of justice
And the sword of change.
Listen to My words and I will bring you healing
*   and peace.*

Let My commands travel deeply into your soul,
And light will enter into darkness.
For I am the dawn, the Mother of Morning Light,
And I will renew your soul.
In love and power I say
Be brave, and prepare for change,
Knowing that the shadow's time is at an end."

Say, "Hail, Diana!" and bow your head. In the next part of this rite, respond to her commands. Take as much time as you need to answer each one. See the goddess before you. You will be lighting seven candles, one for each command.

Light the first candle on the left. Hear Diana speak:

"Embrace the memory of your experience.
Do not be afraid."

Explore the memories that have continued to disturb you. Remember them, feel them. Write down key words from each situation.

Light the candle to the right of the first. Hear her speak:

> *"Let every hurt rise up from the pool of darkness,*
> *And I will take them from you."*

Review each situation again. For each hurt, allow the pain to rise up like a cloud. See it drift up and away from you. Let Diana take it, transform it into light, and then disperse it. Do this for each thing you have listed. Let the process take as long as you need. This is important work, so do not rush. See, feel, release. Add incense to the coal as you feel it is needed.

Light the third candle. Take up the metal or ceramic bowl and the paper that you have written on. Holding one edge of the paper, light a corner. Let it burn, holding it as long as you can; then drop it into the bowl. If a small corner remains unburned, use the tongs to pick it up and relight it, or, if it is very small, place it on the censer coal.

Sprinkle incense on the coal, light the fourth candle, and hear Diana say:

> *"Bathe in my pool of rest and renewal."*

Visualize a beautiful woodland setting with a small lake or pool of water. Feel yourself glide into comfortable waters of rest and renewal. Float in these waters, allowing your mind to remain blank.

Light the fifth candle. Hear her speak again:

> *"Believe in your goodness and strength.*
> *Forgive your imperfections."*

See yourself rise up from her waters of renewal. Forgive your imperfections. Feel your own goodness and strength begin to radiate from you.

Light the sixth candle.

> "Understand the weakness of others.
> Forgive them their imperfections."

Call to mind those who caused you pain. Forgive them their imperfections. Place them in the hands of the Goddess.

Light the seventh candle. Hear her voice:

> "Soon to bed, and to restful sleep.
> I will watch over you tonight,
> O brave soul who is full of courage.
> To sleep, and blessed dreams attend you,
> O much-honored votary."

Immediately following the rite, take a bath in which you have placed a handful of Epsom salts, let the candle burn down, and then go to bed. The next morning, take a spade and dig a hole outside. Bury the ash from the burned paper and anything that is left of the censer coal. Cover this with soil, and then stamp the soil firmly with your feet, saying:

> Fire turned to ashes,
> Ashes buried in Earth,
> Diana, the morning light,
> I, the dawn of rebirth!

3

For Prosperity
and Success

THE ENCHANTMENT OF SRI LAKSHMI

For prosperity

In this rite you will invoke the East Indian Goddess of Good Fortune, Sri Lakshmi. Her golden blessings will enter into your life as you open the pathway of relationship between you and her. Deities that traditionally accompany her also appear in this rite: Saraswati, Goddess of the Arts and of Wisdom, and Ganesha, the Elephant-Headed God who removes obstacles.

ITEMS NEEDED A vase of flowers (with an additional flower added to the vase on the second and third night); a fruit offering; sweet dessert cakes or a bowl of rice; three red taper candles (one for each night of the ritual); and sandalwood stick incense and a censer.

THE ALTAR Arrange the fruit offering, flowers, sweet dessert cakes or rice, and censer on the altar. Have the incense ready. Place the candle in the center of the altar toward the front.

TIMING AND INSTRUCTIONS The duration of this rite is three nights, to be held any time between the new moon and full moon. Cut the incense into two-inch-long sticks. Add an additional flower to the vase on the second and third night.

BODY OF RITUAL At your altar, light a piece of the incense, place it in the censer, and begin, saying:

> *Sri Lakshmi,*
> *Delight of the Earth,*
> *You rose from the waters,*
> *A single lotus in your hand.*

57

> *Golden crowned and brightly jeweled,*
> *Palest of ivory skin and dark doe-eyed,*
> *You are the transcendent divinity of good fortune.*
> *Adorned with many garlands,*
> *Sumptuous veils are draped about you,*
> *Sheer and glittering,*
> *As from your palms*
> *You pour your riches onto the world.*
>
> *Come, Lady, enchant my life with your powers.*
> *Bring good fortune unto me,*
> *And fill my days with your blessings.*

Visualize Lakshmi before you and bow your head. Raise the censer and acknowledge her with fragrant smoke. Set the censer down, saying:

> *Lakshmi, you sit upon your lotus throne*
> *With Lord Ganesha, Remover of Obstacles at your*
>   *right,*
> *And Sri Saraswati, Mother of Wise Arts at your left,*
> *You are the clear path to wise and successful*
>   *prosperity.*

Visualize Ganesha to the right of Lakshmi. Raise the censer and acknowledge him with fragrant smoke. See Saraswati to the left of Lakshmi and acknowledge her with fragrant smoke. Set the censer down and continue:

> *Mother, I ask for your divine blessing.*
> *Let your essence flow,*
> *Making of my life an enchantment of prosperity,*
> *Blessing my new path,*
> *With long-enduring good fortune,*

Adding to it, the delights of health and joy,
As I humbly bow to your holy presence.

Light another piece of incense and place it into the censer. Visualize Lakshmi straight ahead of you. Pick up the incense stick and cense a path between the two of you. Trace the fragrant smoke from you to her, down, and then back to you in a long oval pathway. Do this repeatedly, with a smooth and flowing line. Feel that you are opening a pathway and creating a connection between the Goddess and you.

Light the candle, saying:

Lakshmi, may thy blessings enter into my life,
As I bow to you.

Place the palms of your hands together with your thumbs pressing against your chest over your heart. Bow your head and bring your hands, still in prayer position, up and touch your forehead, then your lips. Lay your hands in your lap.

Again envision a path between you and the Goddess. See the goddess stand and raise her hands as golden glittering light pours out from her palms to you. Feel the light encircle you and move around and through you. Receive it. Say several times, establishing a rhythm:

In golden light, enchantment grows,
Good fortune flows unto me.

Take up the candle and trace the path between you and Lakshmi with the flame. Say repeatedly:

In golden light, enchantment grows,
Good fortune flows unto me.

Then say:

> *By her divine blessings,*
> *The shining light of good fortune is with me.*
> *So be it.*

Let the candle burn down completely. Repeat this ritual for the following two nights.

THE NINE KNOTS OF JUPITER

For beneficence and good fortune

The Roman god Jupiter in his aspect of Beneficent Father God can influence your life by moving the tides of good fortune in your direction. Aspects such as luck, or simply being in the right place at the right time, can carry great power. This rite combines candle-magic with knot-magic to bring these forces into your life. Magic for good health is also included in this rite as a companion to good fortune.

ITEMS NEEDED   Three orange candles and one holder; a 45-inch length of drapery cording or other cord; yellow and gold items such as yellow apples, oranges, gold-foil wrapped chocolate "money," a vase of white, yellow, or orange flowers; a bowl of dried figs, whole nutmeg, and almonds; incense of 4 parts ground frankincense resin, 1 part ground cedar or cut cedar shavings (get cedar shavings in a pet store, and then cut finely with scissors), and 1/4 part ground cloves mixed in a small dish; censer and censer coal.

THE ALTAR   Place one candle in the center front of the altar. Arrange all other items on altar, reserving the remaining two candles for later.

TIMING AND INSTRUCTIONS   Perform the rite two nights before the full moon. As you tie the knots, make sure to leave room for all nine. The next night you will light the second candle. On the full moon, you will light the third candle and untie the knots. Light the censer coal a few minutes before the rite.

BODY OF RITUAL   Light the incense coal. Blow on the embers, then chant:

Jovis Pater, beneficent father,
Bring to me good fortune.
Jovis Pater, beneficent lord,
Bring grace to me now and hereafter.

Light the candle and say:

Jupiter, all-powerful God,
Bringer of good luck and fortunate circumstance,
I call you to my rite!
Pour your gifts into my life,
Moving the tides of fortune,
So that all that comes to me
Is of helpful and beneficent influence.

Pick up the cord. Run it three times over the candle flame, saying:

By Jupiter shall this cord be blessed,
His gifts bound unto its essence.

Place a small amount of incense on the coal. Run the cord three times through the fragrant smoke. State to the God your need for good luck in general or for a particular matter. Place the cord around your neck so that the ends hang down in the front like an untied tie. Chant the following three times:

I shall bind the power of knots in time
The power bound in league times nine,
The spell to be cast by knots in trine,
By three times three luck shall be mine.

Imagine that you are breathing in the powerful golden energies of Jupiter. Envision that each exhale sparkles. Feel his power around you, supporting and assisting you.

Tie the first knot at the end of the cord, but leave the knot loose. Hold the cord up with the open knot before you and breathe in golden Jovian energy. Exhale sparkling light onto the first knot, and silently think: *"Here is the power of the God, of great Jupiter."*

Pull the knot tight. As you pull, visualize that you are capturing the power of the words in the knot.

Loosely tie the second knot. Breathe in golden Jovian energy. Exhale sparkling light onto the knot as you think, *"Jupiter brings me glory and bright fortune."*

Pull the knot tight. As you pull, visualize capturing the power of the words in the knot.

Loosely tie a third knot. Breathe in golden Jovian energy. Exhale sparkling light onto the knot as you think, *"The lord of wealth blesses me with perfect timing."*

Pull the knot tight, capturing the power of the words in the knot.

Loosely tie the fourth knot. Breathe in golden Jovian energy. Exhale sparkling light onto the knot as you think, *"Into my life he brings treasures of delight."*

Pull the knot tight, capturing the power of the words in the knot.

Loosely tie the fifth knot. Breathe in golden Jovian energy. Exhale sparkling light onto the knot as you think, *"Goodness and grace flow to me."*

Pull the knot tight, capturing the power of the words in the knot.

Loosely tie the sixth knot. Breathe in golden Jovian energy. Exhale sparkling light onto the knot, thinking, *"My life is blessed with golden good luck."*

Pull the knot tight, capturing the power of the words in the knot.

Loosely tie the seventh knot. Breathe in golden Jovian energy. Exhale sparkling light onto the knot and think, *"The God of beneficence brings me good health."*

Pull the knot tight, capturing the power of the words in the knot.

Loosely tie the eighth knot. Breathe in golden Jovian energy. Exhale sparkling light onto the knot as you think, *"Wondrous good fortune enters my life."*

Pull the knot tight, capturing the power of the words in the knot.

Loosely tie the ninth knot. Breathe in golden Jovian energy. Exhale sparkling light onto the knot as you think, *"This spell's alive, the power mine!"*

Pull the knot tight, capturing the power of the words in the knot. Visualize the whole cord coming alight and alive with golden light. With both hands, hold up the knotted cord and say:

> *The power bound in league times nine,*
> *This spell is cast by knots in trine.*
> *By Jupiter's cord*
> *What's done is mine.*

On the altar, encircle the candle with the cord, keeping a couple of inches of space between the cord and candle. Sprinkle incense on the censer coal. Let the candle burn down completely.

The Next Night

Light a new orange candle, saying:

> *The power bound in league times nine,*
> *By Jupiter's cord, what's done is mine.*

Let the candle burn down completely.

Night of the Full Moon

Light the third new orange candle, saying:

Hail, Jupiter! Bring your great powers
Unto the culmination of this rite!
Illuminate this magic with your grace;
Come, let thy will and power bless my life.

Take up the cord, and say:

Great Jupiter,
Who brings glory and good fortune,
Who blesses me with perfect timing
And with treasures of delight,
Bring me goodness and grace,
As golden good luck comes to me.
Bless me, too, with good health,
As sparkling good fortune enters into my life!

Slowly untie each knot one by one, envisioning golden, sparkling light seeping out from each one. See the God's power bless you as it enters your life. Let this light of the magic surround you, changing your aura into one that is blessed and ready to receive good fortune. Know that positive opportunity, luck, and good fortune are with you now. Thank the God and ask that he remain with you. Lay the untied cord around the candle and let the candle burn down completely.

TO THE MAIDEN ARTEMIS

For success in an endeavor

This rite invokes the powers of the Greek huntress and virgin moon goddess Artemis. She will bring focus and clarity to you. With the power of her bow you will aim clearly at your dream, achieve your goal, and bring it into your life.

ITEMS NEEDED   Goddess statue or image or a lit pillar candle; sweet pea, lily, or other sweet, lightly scented oil; one white candle and holder; one incense coal; myrrh resin; a censer; white flowers; and a cloth to wipe hands of scented oil.

THE ALTAR   Arrange above items on the altar. Keep the hand-cloth next to the altar.

TIMING AND INSTRUCTIONS   The duration of this rite is one night or one pre-dawn morning between the new moon and the first quarter. Light the coal fifteen minutes before the rite.

BODY OF RITUAL   Place a little myrrh on the censer coal. Raise the smoking censer up in homage to Artemis, saying, *"Hail, Artemis!"* Waft the fragrant smoke across the altar, then say:

> *I call upon Artemis,*
> *Queen of Earth and Heaven*
> *Fair maiden and keen-eyed huntress!*
> *Yours is the wisdom of the wild woodlands.*
> *In silent primordial instinct you act,*
> *Knowing that in action, lies success.*
> *Compassionate Mother of All that Lives,*
> *Hear me, for I seek your aid.*
>
> *Cry of the hawk at midday,*
> *Wide eyes of the watching owl,*

Song of the robin at dawn,
Artemis come unto this rite!
O mistress of fair and holy magic,
Hear my prayer.

With an open heart, explain to her what you desire. Ask her to bless and assist you. Anoint the candle with the scented oil while repeating *"Blessings of Artemis."*

Light the candle saying:

Goddess of unending strength,
Aim thy bow and change my life.
Bless me with your power,
That I may have you with me,
In my body and spirit.
Assist me; may my desire come to be.

Sprinkle more incense on the coal, and say:

Artemis, by your power shall my vision manifest,
And my dream come to fruition!
By your power shall all lead to joy,
In my soul, in my house, and in my life!

Raise your hands to receive her blessing and say:

May she who is both Mother and Maiden, bless me.
May she crown all with health and good fortune.
Come, Artemis, aim thy bow and change my life.

Visualize your desired goal in its completion. Then, see the Goddess draw her bow and aim toward your goal; as she aims, see her face. Watch as the arrow is released, as it hits its mark and melts into golden and silver light. See that light moving through your vision; see yourself in the vision, also immersed in

that light. Suspend yourself in that light for a few moments.
Then say:

> Bright Artemis, praises unto you,
> As I honor the maiden of the silver bow.
> So it is, and ever shall be.

Anoint the insides of your wrists, the insides of your ankles,
and your chest over your heart with the scented oil, saying,
"Blessed by Artemis."

Let the candle burn down completely.

TO THE QUEEN OF FATE

For luck and good fortune

In this spell the Goddess is called upon in three forms: as the Queen of Fate, the Roman Bona Fortuna (good fortune), and the Greek Nemesis (destiny). They will help you weave the threads of fate as you call for a life of good fortune and a destiny well lived.

ITEMS NEEDED   A Goddess statue or image or a lit pillar candle; a small bowl containing equal parts powdered ginger, dried crushed mint, and cedar dust or shavings; one yellow or gold candle, one red candle, and one white candle, and three candle holders; an assortment of yellow, orange, and red fruit; three incense coals and a censer; and three lengths of ribbon (hereafter referred to as *strands* or *threads*) each one yard long, in yellow-gold, red, and white.

THE ALTAR   Arrange the above items on the altar. Place Goddess statue, image, or lit pillar candle in the center of the altar.

TIMING AND INSTRUCTIONS   The duration of this rite is one night, any night between the new moon and the full moon. Light the censer coal fifteen minutes before the rite.

BODY OF RITUAL   Place a small amount of incense onto the lit censer coal. Raise the smoking censer toward your Goddess image in homage, then set it down and say:

> *I stand and face the Queen of Fate,*
> *Sometimes appearing as Bona Fortuna,*
> *Mother of Good Fortune,*
> *Sometimes appearing as Nemesis,*
> *Mother of Destiny.*

I leave behind a past of uncertainty,
As I call forward the destiny of a life well-lived.
I take hold of the reins of my life,
As I call good luck and good fortune into my days.

Sprinkle more incense on the coal and say:

Lady of Good Fortune, prepare the path of my life,
The days and the seasons,
And all events, meetings, and activities great and
  small,
With all of the beauty, joy, and abundance at your
  command.
Weave kindness too, with the Fates,
Into the fabric of my life.

Pick up the three strands of ribbon and drape them over the palm of one hand. Say:

Here lie three threads of fate:
The gold of good fortune,
The red of pleasure,
And the white of peace.

Hold the threads. Imagine the Lady of Good Fortune before you. Say:

O Queen of Fate and Fortune, bless the threads of my
  life.
Fill my days with simple pleasures and satisfactions,
And at every choice and turn I must make,
Be with me, guiding me and showering me
With golden good fortune, and with a heart of peace.
Let the beauties of paradise fill my life,

As the Light of Spirit enters into my experience,
For I choose to tread the path of peace and
  contentment.

Drape the strands around your neck, with both sides hanging
down over your chest. Say:

As the precious days move forward,
With your blessings, I will fulfill my destiny.
Lady, enter into the wheel of my life,
For I am ready to receive the joys,
That your blessings can bring.

Take the gold strand and lay it around the yellow candle. Light
the candle saying, *"Mother of Good Fortune, bring to me perfect
prosperity."*

Lay the red strand around the red candle. Light it and say,
"Mother of Good Fortune, bring to me perfect success."

Lay the white strand around the white candle. Light it and
say, *"Mother of Good Fortune, bring to me perfect peace."*

Pass your hands quickly over each candle flame. Carefully
remove the threads. Tie them together at one end, leaving several inches behind the knot. Hold your hands before the candle
flames and say:

May the Weaver of Destiny enter,
And work through these hands.

Braid the strands together. Bring the three candles together in a
small circle. Wind the braid loosely around the three candles. Say:

Pleasant days, good fortune, and sweet contentment
Shall enter my life.
I praise the Queen of Fate.

Sprinkle incense on the censer coal. As the candle burns down, bow your head, tie the braid loosely around your neck, and wear it overnight. Then place it beside your bed for one week. Later, store it in a special place, or under your altar. Eat a portion of the fruit now and finish the remainder of it over the next few days.

THE POWER OF HERMES

For success in a business venture

Hermes the Greek Messenger God was first the protector and guardian of wayfarers. Later he became the God of Commerce and the marketplace. Even later, great powers of magic were ascribed to him. He brought success to business ventures and even became a favorite of orators and writers. In the following rite using candle-magic, a wand, and fragrant smoke, you will invoke him, calling his powers into your life so that success will be yours.

ITEMS NEEDED   Three white taper candles; one part oil of bergamot diluted with a half-part olive oil; six feathers; a dried (not green) small branch with twigs and leaves removed to make a slender wand; an incense burner, censer coal, and incense of 2 parts ground frankincense, 2 parts pine sawdust or ground pine bark, and 1/2 part dried and crushed mint.

THE ALTAR   Arrange two of the taper candles on the right and left of your altar toward the rear. Place one of the candles in the center of the altar with three feathers arranged on its right side and three on the left. Lay the wand in front of the center candle. Place the remaining items on the altar.

TIMING AND INSTRUCTIONS   The duration of this rite is one night and may be held any time between the new moon to the full moon. Light the censer coal several minutes before the rite. Before you begin, think of several affirmations for your success. Write them down and keep them near your altar in case you need to refer to them during the rite.

BODY OF RITUAL   Light the left and right candles. Anoint the tip of the wand with the bergamot oil. Sprinkle a little incense on the coal and say:

> Hail, Hermes!
> Winged god born on Mount Cyllene.
> Heraldic messenger, diviner of fates,
> Once mischievous, child of the goddess Maia,
> You are knowledge, wisdom, letters, magic,
> And all successful enterprise!
> Hermes! Winds whistle and cry out,
> Wings flutter, and a flash of gold glints across the
>   skies
> As the Lord of Magic comes to me.

Light the center candle and sprinkle incense on the coal. Say:

> Long-winged and white are your sacred birds.
> Your cranes surround you, while graceful and strong
> You rise among them, staff in hand.
> Winged sandals of gold carry you swift as the wind.
> From your heavenly domain you call out,
> Speaking my name, drawing my spirit into the skies,
> Hermes, I rise to your power.
> I am drawn to you who are clarity and knowledge.

Sprinkle more incense on the coal. Begin to speak with Hermes and tell him about your goal. Hear him affirm your goal for you. See his cranes circle you.

Pick up your wand and dip the end in bergamot or mint oil. Let it sit in the oil for a moment, then light the end of the wand in the center candle's flame. Write the following words in the air in flame and smoke: "By the power of Hermes."

Be sure the wand flame is completely extinguished, and dip the wand tip again in oil and flame. Then write a personal statement of your success in the air. When needed you may relight the end of the wand.

End by saying:

> *By the power of Hermes,*
> *Shall . . . [state your goal here]*
> *Succeed and prosper.*
> *By the power of Hermes,*
> *Shall this be so, with joy and pleasure*
> *As bright companions to my success.*
> *Praise and honor to Hermes.*
> *I give thanks to he who is agile and swift in his*
>   *powers.*
> *So be it.*

Sprinkle more incense on the coal. Let the candles burn down completely.

By the Lady's Blessing

For successful employment

This rite invokes the Great Mother, who in her wisdom and compassion will find the right work for you. You will use the sacred circle to enter into the sphere of her power. With candle-magic and light-visioning, you will be brought together with your ideal employment as each night of the spell unfolds.

ITEMS NEEDED   Seven apples and five almonds; a mixture of 1 part cyclamen or lily oil and 1 part olive oil; a piece of jewelry you have worn often; five white candles; and a dish of fresh rose petals.

THE ALTAR   Arrange the five candles in a circle on your altar. Outside this circle place a circle of apples. Inside the candle circle, place a point-up star of five almonds. Have ready on the altar the jewelry, dish of rose petals, and the oil.

TIMING AND INSTRUCTIONS   The duration of this rite is one night with follow-up activities for five days. After the rite, let the candles burn down fully. You will be eating the apples and almonds and wearing the piece of jewelry used in the rite in the days following the rite. When you find employment, give thanks to the Lady.

Begin by anointing insides of your ankles and wrists with scented oil while saying, *"By the Lady's blessing, I call success into my life."* Then say:

> *Holy Mother,*
> *In your great wisdom,*
> *Choose for me the perfect labor,*

That employment by which I shall live
Happily upon this Earth.

Many are the wanderings of my mind,
By which I have sought to know
The path that holds success for me.
And so, I call upon your miraculous ways,
To bring unto me the perfect employment.

Envision a circle of light around you. See the Goddess's arms encircle you. Feel her warm, comforting rose-colored light; her white and silver light of purity; her violet-blue light of magic and power. Visualize a circle of violet-blue around your ring of unlit candles. Then say:

Here is her Circle of Power,
And it is awake with light.
Into it I place a personal adornment,
So that it shall enter into her Circle of Power.

Place the jewelry into the candle circle. Say:

Into this circle I place the sweet petals of the rose,
So that beauty and goodness will be with me
In my endeavor.

Place the rose petals into the circle. Say:

Into this circle I breathe the breath of life,
So that the magic shall awaken.

Raise energy up from the Earth through your feet, rising up through you as silver-white light. Purse your lips and breathe light into the circle. Then say:

All-powerful Mother of Life,
Guide me now to the perfect work,

> *One with greater prosperity than I have known,*
> *With happy surroundings*
> *And pleasant coworkers.*

Take a slow, deep breath, visioning that you are drawing in energizing light. Let it fill your body. Starting with the candle on the far side of the ring, light them, moving in a clockwise direction. As you light each one say:

> *By her power I shall succeed;*
> *Prosperity in harmony,*
> *The perfect work, it comes to me;*
> *And so . . . it . . . shall . . . be!*

After all of the candles are lit, say:

> *Great Mother, I place this in your hands.*
> *For it is with your power that I shall succeed.*
> *And so, I now release my need,*
> *Into your compassionate hands.*
> *So be it.*

Take a small step back from the altar and release any excess energy with a big exhale. Bend at your waist and allow your arms, head, and torso to dangle; lie down on the floor. Feel your connection to the Earth. Ground the energy by releasing it all into the Earth. Allow your mind to relax, clear, and be still. Let everything go. When you are finished, have something to eat.

For five days following the rite, eat one of the apples and one of the almonds in the morning. Wear the piece of jewelry all day. Place the remaining two apples outside.

4

For Blessings
and New Beginnings

HESTIA'S FLAME

Rite for a house blessing

Hestia, the Greek Goddess of Hearth and Home, is called upon to bless your living space in this ritual. Your rooms will be purified and Hestia's blessings of spirituality and light will be brought into your home. This rite is particularly useful when moving into a new dwelling.

ITEMS NEEDED   A white candle and holder for each room in your dwelling place; censer, censer coal, tongs, and incense of 2 parts ground frankincense, 2 parts ground myrrh, and 1/4 part ground cinnamon; and a small cup of wine, a portion of bread, and several flowers set on a tray or platter.

THE ALTAR   Set one candle in a holder, the platter of bread, wine, and flowers, and the incense items on your stove in the kitchen.

TIMING AND INSTRUCTIONS   The duration of this rite is one night and can be done at any time of the month. Open one window in each room. The ritual will begin in the kitchen.

BODY OF RITUAL   Light the candle in the kitchen and say:

> Hestia, Goddess of the Sacred Flame
> That burns within the core of all life,
> Whose golden and amber glow,
> Is the spark of the Eternal Spirit,
> Come, and enter here!
>
> Hestia, dwell now in the midst of this home,
> Making of it your own sacred hearth,

Making of it a place where the highest of spirit lives.
Bring the essence of love here,
Creating a strong and lasting home.

Bright Goddess of Heaven and Earth,
Come, send your powers throughout my home,
Cleansing, purifying, and blessing this place
With your ancient fire.

Candle Blessing for Each Room

Begin in the kitchen. Using a pair of tongs, pick up the censer coal. Light it on two sides using the Hestia candle. Blow on the coal gently to help the lighting process, and set it in the censer. Pick up the candle and circle your kitchen in a clockwise direction while holding up the candle flame, saying, *"Hail, Hestia!"* Now take the candle from the kitchen, and go from room to room in your home, moving in as much of a clockwise direction as possible. Light each room's candle with the kitchen candle, saying, *"Hail, Hestia!"*

Incense Blessing for Each Room

Return to the kitchen and set the kitchen candle back down. Sprinkle incense on the lit coal. If the outside of your censer has gotten hot, hold it with oven pads or a folded towel. Pick up the censer, and hold it steady so that the coal does not slide back and forth. Circle your kitchen clockwise with the fragrant smoke, censing a circle around windows and doorways. Complete the censing of each room by stopping in the center of the room and raising the censer up toward the ceiling and then down toward the floor, saying:

By the power of Heaven and Earth,
May Hestia bless this house.
By her eternal and sacred flame,
Here shall light and joy reside.
By her holy hand,
Shall these walls keep us safe,
And protect us throughout day and night
In the name of Hestia,
So be it.

Carry the censer and incense to each room and cense it in the manner described. Place more incense on the coal as needed.

Partaking of the Bread and Wine

Return to the kitchen. Take a little wine and bread and go outside your home and place these offerings on the Earth, saying, *"For Hestia, the first and the last!"* Return to your kitchen and partake of the bread and wine. As you sip the wine, hail her. Follow this with a nice dinner in your kitchen. If you have a pet, give the pet a special meal or treat. Let all candles burn down completely.

INVOCATION OF THE MAIDEN DIANA

For new beginnings

In this rite you will invoke the Roman Goddess Diana, moon maiden and Roman version of Artemis. She will bring you the blessings of a successful new beginning and remain with you until your goal is realized.

ITEMS NEEDED   Three white candles and holders; a vase of flowers in white or pastel colors; and sweet pea, myrrh, or lily oil.

THE ALTAR   Arrange the above on the altar.

INSTRUCTIONS   The duration of rite is one night, to take place just after the new moon or in the first few days of the waxing moon.

BODY OF RITUAL   Anoint yourself with scented oil. Light one candle and say:

> *Hail, Lady of the Silver Crescent,*
> *Diana, who is Maiden, and yet Mother of All,*
> *Come, and attend this rite.*

Light the second candle and say:

> *I praise the Lady of Blossoming Fields;*
> *How perfectly the fragrant lily reflects your beauty.*
> *You rise at every dawn of new beginnings.*
> *You are the magic of all things*
> *As they emerge from creation.*
> *Without you, nothing is born or comes to fruition.*
> *And so I praise and honor you.*
> *Lady, come and hear my prayer.*

Tell Diana your endeavor and ask for her assistance. Then light the third candle, saying:

> *May Diana bless my endeavor.*
> *And lend her powers unto my spirit.*
> *May she bring me success and good fortune*
> *And stay with me until all comes to fruition.*
> *Lady, I honor you and give you my fervent thanks,*
> *Saying, Hail, Diana!*
> *And Blessed Be!*

Let the candles burn down completely.

THE PROMISSORY OATH

To achieve a goal

Making an oath was a common practice in ancient Greece, because the completion of that which you've sworn to do brings the favor of the Gods. In this ritual you choose the deities, either three deities that you are already familiar with or three that you wish to learn about. Through this ritual you will create a spiritual agreement by which you gain divine blessings.

ITEMS NEEDED   Three votive candles in holders; seven white taper candles with one of them in a holder; offerings for each deity; stick incense and holder; several sheets of paper and a pen; and one yard of ribbon.

THE ALTAR   Arrange the votive candles in the center of altar in front of the taper candle in the holder. Place the incense on the altar. Deity images or statues are nice decorations but are optional. Have the paper, pen, ribbon, and offerings ready beside the altar.

TIMING AND INSTRUCTIONS   The duration of this rite is one night of ritual plus six nights of candle lighting, and may be performed at any lunar phase. Choose which three deities you will ask for aid and decide on a service or donation to be performed in the name of each deity. Follow through on these after the rite. Note: Customize this rite to fit the deities you've chosen. The words in brackets are those you can replace with your own.

BODY OF THE RITUAL   Light the central taper candle. Pick up the paper and pen, and begin by writing:

> *May the Goddesses [Gods] attend my oath,*
> *See my commitment,*
> *Receive my offerings and praises,*
> *And grant me their blessings.*

Light the incense and write:

> *I call upon [Artemis, Athena, and Hecate]*
> *And ask for your aid,*
> *Empower me to achieve my goal.*
> *And for this blessing,*
> *I shall give of my time and resources in the following*
>   *way[s]*

Now write your commitments you've chosen on the paper. Then write, "*For [Artemis, Athena, and Hecate] I bring the offerings [list the offerings you've brought].*"

Now light a votive candle for each deity, saying each deity's name as you light each candle. Place their offerings on the altar. Write: "*And to each I offer honorable praises.*"

Write a sentence of praise for each one. Then say, "*Powerful Goddesses [or Gods], come and grant my blessing.*"

Begin asking for your blessings by writing, "*May Artemis, Athena, and Hecate grant that I . . .*" Then follow this with writing the blessings you wish to receive.

Then say:

> *By [Artemis, Athena, and Hecate],*
> *I will keep my oath.*
> *May the Goddesses [Gods] grant me health and long life,*
> *And the blessings that I seek,*
> *As I honor them.*
> *So be it.*

Kiss the written pages. Roll the oath up, tie it with the ribbon, and set it on the altar. Let the candles burn down completely.

The next night, remove the votive candle holders. Light another white taper candle, setting the oath in front of it. Continue lighting a white taper candle each night in front of the oath for a total of seven nights. Be sure you keep your commitments.

THE BLESSINGS OF DUIR

For the blessing of holy objects

Among the Celts and their priests the Druids, the Sacred Oak is called Duir. Duir is the King of High Summer. Oneness, strength, endurance, high spirituality, and magic are all the qualities of Duir. In the rite that follows, ritual objects, jewelry, or other small personal items may be blessed with his power.

ITEMS NEEDED   One white votive candle in a holder; a censer and incense of your choice; a cup of water; a bowl of grain; a table or inverted crate covered with fabric for a small altar, enough dried oak leaves to surround the altar in a circle of leaves; a small oak branch eight to ten inches in length; scissors; 1 yard of green ribbon for each object to be blessed; and a cloth upon which you will set the objects.

THE ALTAR   On the altar, place the censer and the oak branch in the east, the bowl of grain in the north, the cup of water in the west, and the candle in the south.

TIMING AND INSTRUCTIONS   The duration of this rite is one night, to take place anytime between the new and full moon. Place the cloth on the ground next to the altar and place the objects to be blessed on the cloth. (If the objects are small, you may place them in the center of the altar.) The circle blessing below and the consecrations are based on traditional Wiccan blessings.

Casting the Circle

Walk clockwise in a circle around the altar sprinkling the oak leaves as you go. Say:

Circle of oak, where thou art cast,
No harm nor adverse purpose pass,
But in complete accord with me,
For good I will it,
So mote it be!

Invocation

Light the incense and pick up the oak branch. Say:

We call upon Duir,
The power of the oak.
Ancient forest of towering oak,
Thick your great canopy of weaving branches,
Hardy, the green of precious leaves.
You endure through fire, flood, and drought
To rise again with beauty in the new season.

You have been the timber of mighty ships,
Taking great nations to new lands,
And changing the course of history.
You are also the bounty of generosity,
Your golden acorns providing abundant food.

O sacred tree of midsummer,
To the learned Druids your name means the door.
Best are you to build the entrance to home and
*   hearth.*
And in the realm of spirit, Duir in all matters
Means the way to strength, knowledge, and triumph.

Therefore I call upon you,
O spirit of the ancient forests,
I call upon you to enter this circle.

Place the branch on the altar, light the candle, and say:

> With the powers of the oak,
> I wish to consecrate this [name the object]
> With the blessings of Duir.

Tie the objects with green ribbon so that they may be held up. (If the objects are rings, tie them together.)

Blessing the Objects

You will be holding the objects over each of the elements for the blessings.

Go to the east side of the altar. Hold the objects over the censer smoke and say:

> By the powers of this fragrant smoke,
> Be these [objects] sanctified,
> Sacred smoke, creature of air,
> Bless these [objects]
> So that they will bring the highest and best in their
>   holy use,
> In the name of Duir.
> And so it is.

Move to the south side of the altar. Hold the objects over the candle flame and say:

> By the power of this sacred flame,
> Be these [objects] purified,
> Now is any dross dispelled,
> Now does all good enter herein,
> In the name of Duir,
> And so it is.

Move to the west side of the altar. Sprinkle the objects with
water and say:

> *By the power of this sacred water,*
> *Be these [objects] consecrated,*
> *With divine strength, joy, and success,*
> *In the name of Duir,*
> *And so it is.*

Move to the north side of the altar. Hold the objects above the
grain and say:

> *By the power of our mother the earth,*
> *And in the name of Duir,*
> *May these [objects]*
> *Bring blessings of beauty, health, and longevity*
> *To those who use them.*
>
> *Great praises to the sacred oak,*
> *All honor to Duir.*
> *So be it.*

Wrap the objects and store them until they need to be used.

5

For Love
and Friendship

THE BLESSINGS OF ISHTAR

To bring romantic love into your life

This ritual invokes the Babylonian goddess Ishtar, Mother of Earth and Queen of Heaven. In this rite we will call upon her as Mistress of Love to allow her to bring you the perfect match. Through candle-magic and self-anointing with fragrant oil, you will call love into your life.

ITEMS NEEDED   Four red candles and four holders; rose oil; a censer and two 2-inch pieces of sandalwood stick incense; a vase of pink or red roses with greenery; and a bowl of fresh rose petals.

THE ALTAR   Arrange the four candles in a diamond shape in the center of the altar. Set the bowl of rose petals, the rose oil, and the censer on the altar. Cut one stick of sandalwood incense in half and set it on the altar.

TIMING AND INSTRUCTIONS   The duration of this rite is one night and can be held any time between the new and full moon. This rite will not draw a specific person to you; it is designed to request the Goddess to provide the one who is the perfect love for you.

BODY OF RITUAL   Light one of the pieces of stick incense. Pick it up and cense your altar. Place it into the censer. Bow your head and open your heart to the Goddess. Say:

> *Hail, Ishtar!*
> *Enchanting mistress of love and pleasure,*
> *Honey-sweet Goddess of the Sacred Bed,*

> From your body you bestow your gifts
> Upon the naked human soul,
> Bringing warmth, love, and affection.
>
> O Lady of Life and Creation,
> From whose heart arise gardens of paradise,
> Come, and bring to me love's mysteries.
>
> From your crown of soft-petaled roses,
> Fragrant petals fall with every step,
> As wisdom and beauty stream from thy holy presence.
> Glittering in gold and amber adornments
> You shall forever remain the Great Queen of Babylon.
>
> And so I bow,
> And with praises call upon you.
> I pray that love will blossom as the spirit soars,
> And that passion will rise
> As your powers ripen into ecstasy.
> And may the one that you bring to me,
> Care for me not only with passion,
> But with a kind heart.

Sprinkle rose petals around the unlit candles and say:

> Ishtar . . . you know the longings of my heart
>   and soul,
> And so I call upon you in my time of need.

Anoint a spot on your chest over your heart with rose oil
and say:

> Perfect and unfolding is the rose of my heart.
> Waiting only for the gift of sacred loving.
> By your unending powers
> May this precious gift enter into my life.

Light the first candle, at the back of the altar, and say:

> *Through you*
> *Who makes the stars shine in the Heavens,*
> *Shall my beloved come to me.*

Light the second candle, at the right of the first, and say:

> *Through you*
> *Who makes riches flow across the land,*
> *Shall my beloved come to me.*

Light the third candle and say:

> *Through you*
> *Who brings joy to sacred lovers,*
> *Shall my beloved come to me.*

Light the fourth candle and say:

> *Through you*
> *Who brings love's comfort to heart and soul,*
> *Shall my beloved come to me.*

Light a second piece of incense and say:

> *Praises to Ishtar*
> *Who grants love's bright benedictions.*
> *And so it shall be.*

Waft fragrant smoke over the candles. Set the incense back in the censer. Let the candles burn down completely. The next day scatter the rose petals outside saying, *"Hail, Ishtar!"*

To Fair Kore

To draw loving friends

This rite calls upon the maiden Kore, daughter of the Greek Earth Mother, Demeter. Kore embodies springtime, youthful joy, and innocent play. Her sacred companions provide her with love and trust, the ideals of good friendship. As you call upon Kore, you open a pathway for new friends to come forward and enter your life.

ITEMS NEEDED   A white taper candle and holder; incense of choice and censer; sweet pea, rose, lily, or myrrh oil; a tool with a fine point, such as a knife or a pen; greenery, a vase of multi-colored flowers, and a basket or bowl of additional multicolored flowers to be used for offerings; and a small towel or cloth.

THE ALTAR   Place the candle in the center of the altar. Surround it with greenery. Place the bottle of fragrant oil, the vase of flowers, and the tool on the altar. Keep the other items adjacent to altar.

TIMING AND INSTRUCTIONS   The duration of this rite is one night and can be held any time between the new moon and first quarter. Just before the rite is enacted, prepare the candle. Carve the word *Kore* on it four times. Anoint the candle and wick with scented oil saying, *"To bring friendship."*

BODY OF RITUAL   Light the incense and say:

> *Pure and holy maiden,*
> *Fair offspring of the Great Mother*
> *Whose countenance speaks of sunlit days*
> *And dewy flowers,*
> *Whose smile fills the heart with joy and unending*
>   *love,*
> *O hear my prayer.*

Light the candle and say:

> *Never do you desire*
> *For one single soul to feel alone.*
> *But ever do you wish the blessings of*
> *Pleasant companionship and loving friendship*
> *Upon each son and daughter of the Great Mother.*
> *And so, in my need*
> *I call upon your tender heart*
> *And ask for your blessing.*

Anoint the center of your forehead and a spot above your heart with fragrant oil and say:

> *Kore, bring into the patterns of my life,*
> *One who is trustworthy, honest, and kind,*
> *One who may come to understand my spirit,*
> *As I may come to understand theirs.*

Scatter the flowers around the candle. Visualize the Maiden attending you. See her place her hands above your head, showering you with silver and white light. She gives you her blessings. Say:

> *Holy Maiden,*
> *Bring new friendship into my life.*
> *May comradeship and joy run free;*
> *May friendship attend me.*
>
> *Into the great Web of Life,*
> *You send your power.*
> *Purpose, thought, and magic flow;*
> *The pathway has opened.*
> *May all that is good flow to me.*

Envision her standing behind you with her arms extended. See Kore and yourself together in a luminous silvery light.

Look at the candle flame. See the energy and light of the flame, extending outward into the many streaming pathways of the Web of Life. Say:

> *Hands reach out as friendship comes,*
> *Hearts reach out, a meeting done.*
> *May all that is good friendship flow to me.*
> *Blessed Be.*

Let the candle burn down completely. The next day, scatter the flowers that surrounded the candle outside. Keep fresh flowers on your altar for one week.

PRAYER TO MARY OF THE SACRED HEART

For love and compassion

For millions of people around the world, Mary is the Compassionate Mother who is honored, worshiped, and prayed to for every need. She is available to all, regardless of religious affiliation. Many miracles have been attributed to her. She is the Divine Mother, whose origins are Mari of the Chaldeans and Mariham of the Persians. Embracing all, gentle and kindhearted, Mary listens, provides comfort, and bestows her compassionate love.

ITEMS NEEDED   An icon or image of Mary; three white candles and one holder; incense and a censer; and a vase of flowers.

THE ALTAR   Arrange above items on your altar as you wish.

TIMING AND INSTRUCTIONS   The duration of this rite is three nights and to be held during any lunar phase.

BODY OF RITUAL   Light the incense and the candle and say:

> *Gentle Mother,*
> *How beautiful and sweet you are.*
> *Your light is everywhere.*
> *There is no place it cannot shine.*
> *Through you does confusion transform into a blessed*
>   *sea of tranquillity.*
> *Through you are miracles of all kinds brought to pass.*
>
> *Sacred Mother of sweetness and simplicity,*
> *You shine your power*
> *Into the thousands of worldly possibilities;*
> *Into the heart of the innocent,*
> *Into the heart of the doubter,*

Into the heart of those who blame and name,
Into the heart of all who love you.
Your power is unending.

Sacred Mother,
I surrender to you,
To your sweetness.
You are honey that flows from my heart.
Mia Mater,
Light of compassion,
Hail!

Let the incense and candle burn down completely. Repeat ritual for two more nights.

TO INANNA, MOTHER OF SUMER

To receive her healing love

This ritual invokes Sumerian Inanna, who has many various powers. As a Mother Goddess, her strength can heal the broken heart, refresh the spirit, and bring peace to the soul. Using candle-magic and visualizations, you will bring her to you. Her powerful healing love will fill your spirit with a sense of warmth, love, caring, and protection.

ITEMS NEEDED   Three red candles, three purple or lavender candles, and three white candles with three holders; myrrh incense, a censer, and censer coal; a vase containing three red roses for the first night, three pink flowers for the second night, and three white flowers for the third night.

THE ALTAR   Arrange one red, one purple, and one white candle on the altar with the censer and incense. Keep the other items to the side.

TIMING AND INSTRUCTIONS   The duration of this rite is three nights, and can be held anytime between the new and full moon.

BODY OF RITUAL   Light the red candle and the incense. Raise the censer and say:

> *I ask Holy Inanna to be with me now.*
> *Ancient Mother of Sumer,*
> *Crowned with leaves of beaten gold,*
> *Fragrant with myrrh and attar of roses,*
> *You rise before me in beauty and power.*

Place the vase of three red roses on the altar.

> *Where you have stood,*
> *Civilizations have risen and flourished.*

With a gentle word,
Lovers meet and children are born;
While the touch of your hand
Brings gardens of paradise into being.

All things that are born from love,
These, arise from your power.
And so I call upon you.
Come, and touch my heart;
Mend what is broken.
Let your love and warmth descend into my soul.
Nourish my spirit,
And fill my heart with peace.

Light the purple candle and say:

Divine Mother, I am thine.
My heart is filled with love for you.
In peace and protection,
Your power surrounds me,

You are my light of understanding
And I reside with you.
Bless me with your love and transforming powers.
Work your magic, O precious Mother.
As I life safely within your loving arms.

I rest upon your altar of love
And am renewed.

Light the white candle and visualize yourself approaching her. Then rest in her arms like a child, feeling her warmth and powerful protection. You are safe and in her perfect care. Let this last as long as you need. When you are done, say:

Praises to Inanna, Mother of Sumer,
For I am renewed upon her altar of love.

Sprinkle more incense on the coal. Let candles burn down completely.

Repeat the ritual for two nights. Use pink flowers the second night and white flowers the third.

6

For Honorable
Endings and Farewells

Banshee Macha

To end malicious gossip

If someone is speaking about you with malicious intent and will not stop, even though you've tried speaking with the offender, this rite is a solution.

Items Needed   Incense of equal parts ground frankincense, cinnamon, and cedar (or frankincense stick incense); a censer coal; a censer; an unfired clay bowl that you have painted gray; several sheets of newspaper or other paper to be used to wrap the bowl; a large paper bag; a heavy cloth or towel; a bowl of red ink or paint and a small brush (or a fine-tip red marker); and one red, one black, and one white candle, all in holders.

The Altar   Arrange all of the above items on the altar except for the paper and cloth, which are to be set on the floor to the side of the altar.

Timing and Instructions   Hold this rite approximately one week after the full moon.

Body of Ritual   If you're not using stick incense, light the censer coal a few minutes ahead of the rite.

Be seated at your altar. Sprinkle incense on the lit coal or light the stick incense. Say:

> *I call the Morrigan, Mother of the Celts,*
> *O Threefold Goddess of Life, Death, and Rebirth.*
> *Come and attend me in this rite of magic.*

Light the black candle and say:

> *Hail, Morrigan!*
> *As Macha, you are the raven*
> *Hovering above the battlefield,*
> *The blood of slain warriors*
> *Upon thy black feathers.*
> *O Goddess of Death, hear my prayer.*

Light the red candle and say:

> *Taking human form, you are Badba,*
> *Stirring the cauldron of mortal life.*
> *With all of its possibilities.*
> *O Goddess of Life, hear my prayer.*

Light the white candle and say:

> *As Ana, you take the contents*
> *Of the cauldron's spell*
> *And pour it upon the battlefield*
> *Making of all, new human creation.*
> *O Goddess of Rebirth, hear my prayer.*

Place more incense on the coal. Say:

> *I call to the Morrigan, to the three as one.*
> *Come, and bring your powers unto my cause.*
> *Someone has spoken of me,*
> *Not in ways of love, or friendship,*
> *But in the manner of gossip—hurtful, low, and cruel.*
> *Teach them, Great Morrigan, not to do so.*

Point to the gray bowl and say, *"Here is their heart, their ways of gossip."*

Paint their name in red ink on the inside bottom of the bowl. Then say, *"Here is their name upon this ashen bowl."*

Paint a circular line midway around the inside of the bowl. Then paint the names *Ana*, *Badba*, and *Macha*, repeatedly around the upper inside of the bowl. Then say, *"Here are your names, to cleanse their very soul."*

Paint a circle and three red feathers around the person's name. Say:

> *Should they again wish to speak ill of me,*
> *Of my life, or thoughts, or deeds,*
> *Then shall you come as the black Raven,*
> *To teach them your wisdom.*
> *As Banshee Macha, shall you keen and cry out*
> *And make yourself known to them,*
> *In feathers black and glistening,*
> *Does the raven make her presence known.*
>
> *And so they will awake,*
> *To see the unkindness of their own words.*
> *Until they are quiet, within their center core.*
> *So shall you watch them, teach them, guide them,*
> *Unto ways that are noble and good.*
>
> *I give thanks to Banshee Macha,*
> *To the Raven of Ulster,*
> *And to all ravens of morning, noon, and night.*
> *I honor the black raven who guards and protects me,*
> *Now and forever more.*
> *And so it is.*

Wrap the bowl in paper and put it inside the paper bag. Place a heavy cloth or towel down in front of you on the floor. Hold the package and say:

As I break this bowl,
May the power be released
And flow into the Web of Life.

Crash the bowl down onto the cloth saying, *"May Macha guard and protect me!"*

Bury the broken pieces at night. Do not fear the one who gossips any longer. Let it go and leave it to Banshee Macha.

COME KALI-MA

To release pain of the past

This rite heals deep pain of the past. I have used it for victims of rape, which is what it was originally designed for. Kali is very potent and will not fail you.

ITEMS NEEDED   Sandalwood stick incense and holder; one black and one yellow candle in holders; red flowers in a vase; blood-red paint or henna, and a brush; a bell, rattle, or tambourine; flowers for an offering; Epsom salts; and a favorite scented oil.

THE ALTAR   Arrange all of the above items with the black, red, and yellow candles about three inches apart from each other. Have flowers ready at the side of the altar. Place the scented oil and Epsom salts in the bathroom for later use.

TIMING AND INSTRUCTIONS   The duration of this rite is one night, to be done when the moon is waning.

Light the incense and say:

> *Dark and divine,*
> *Blue-black hair streaming,*
> *Heavy-scented, sweet, and haunting,*
> *One moment the fearsome hag*
> *With the look of all ages in her eyes,*
> *One moment the delicate dark Maiden, golden*
> *   anklets jingling.*
> *With gentle laughter, she is Kali-Ma.*

Light the black candle. Say:

> *Kali, I call you to my rite!*
> *Ancient One, yours is the dance of Death.*

*Black-skinned, many armed, with henna-reddened
  palms,
A necklace of white skulls shines against your
  darkness.
Golden bells sway as you move in your mysterious art.*

*Kali! In your sacred dance
You show your great purpose to us all.
For you are Time,
The mistress of endings and beginnings.
And as you dance, Shiva dies and time moves
  forward,
So that he can be born again.*

Ring the bell, or shake the rattle or tambourine in a circle over
the candles. Say:

*Lady, I seek your aid!
I have been joined in life,
To a sorrow of the past,
Tied to my soul is this chain,
Which drags my spirit into darkness.
But the time has come for these bonds to be released.
It is for this that I pray to you tonight.
Great Kali, hear my prayer!*

Place your offering of flowers in front of the candles. Say:

*As life moves forward,
There must be endings.
And so Kali-Ma,
I call you to dance with me upon this old sorrow
Which needs to be released.
Come, Dark One,
Dance this sorrow to its death and its ending.*

Light the red candle and say:

> *Kali, come to me,*
> *And I, as you, with henna-reddened palms*
> *Will dance the dance of Death!*

Paint the centers of your palms blood-red. Hold them above the flame. Say:

> *These are the hands,*
> *This is the body of Kali.*

Breathe her in. See the skulls sway against your black skin. Let your henna-reddened palms dance. Hear your golden bracelets jingle. Consider the wound that you wish to heal. Say:

> *Unwise one who has injured me,*
> *Now shall you feel the power of Kali!*
> *The pain, the wound which is your making*
> *Shall in this dance be returned to you.*
> *What is yours, will return to you!*

Stare into the candle flame, then chant the following over and over, gaining a rhythm as you go. Add a melody if you like.

> *Kali, come to me!*
> *Kali, free me!*
> *Kali-Ma dance . . .*
> *Dance with me!*

When ready, begin the dance of Death. You are Kali-Ma. Continue the chant as above, sway and move your body. Let your body dance in whatever way it wants. As you do so, in your mind's eye see the perpetrator of the wound or injury. Dance upon this image until it falls to pieces and disintegrates into dust. Then say the word *Kali-Ma*. See her name flow out from you as a dark cloud; let it cover the dust that remains of the perpetrator. Say:

> *In the name of Kali,*
> *May this return to the one who injured me!*

See the remains disappear. See the dark cloud of dust dissolve into nothing. Let yourself feel and express whatever you need to. When you are done, bend forward at the waist and release all energies with an exhale. Release, relax. Then say:

> *Unwise one who injured me,*
> *What is yours has returned to you*
> *By way of Kali.*
> *May you learn from her wisdom.*

When you are done, return to your altar. Light incense again if it has gone out. Light the yellow candle and waft incense over it three times. Say:

> *Kali-Ma, your dance is done,*
> *Come shed your black skin*
> *And reveal the golden shining one*
> *Who waits beneath.*

See Black Kali shed her skin like a serpent. Her golden aspect is revealed; her light breaks out like a great sun. Stand up. Feel that you are shedding your black skin, then let your golden light pour forward, and say:

> *Gauri, golden aspect of Mother Kali,*
> *From within me rises*
> *Your sweet powers of renewal.*
> *Your are life, emerging from death*
> *So that I may live in joy again.*

I praise both Kali the Black
And Gauri the Golden!
Praises! And blessed be.

Leave the black candle and the red candle on the altar and move the yellow candle to your sleeping area. Cense your sleeping area with sandalwood.

Next, rinse off in the shower, then bathe in a warm bath of Epsom salts and, if you like, add a few drops of scented oil. Relax in your bath, and see Gauri's golden light all around you.

TO THE ANCIENT CRONE

For the passing on of a pet

We love our animals dearly, but the Fates have decreed that they do not live as long as we do. And so we enjoy, love, and care for them while they are with us. To receive their love is a tremendous blessing, but we must let them go when they die. Their death is one last gift, for they teach us about life and death, and the spirit that is within both.

ITEMS NEEDED   Censer, incense coal, and myrrh incense; one white, one black, and one violet candle, each in a holder; a vase of flowers; and an image of your pet, if you have one.

THE ALTAR   Set the candles up so that they form a triangle with the black one at the point farthest from you with the white and the violet ones marking the other two corner points of the horizontal line of the triangle, which faces you. Arrange the other items as you wish.

TIMING AND INSTRUCTIONS   This rite may be held at any time of the lunar cycle.

BODY OF RITUAL   Light the censer coal five minutes ahead of the ritual. Place incense on the coal and say:

> To the ancient crone,
> Some call you Hecate,
> Others the Morrigan,
> Still others call you simply Dark Mother,
> But I shall call you the Kind Face of Death.
>
> You have presented yourself to one who is beloved to me,
> To my child, my friend, my familiar,
> To one who is as part of my soul.

I know that life does not stand still,
That we live within the skein of time.
Not one of us
Shall live here forever,
And so, through my beloved spirit friend,
Today, I will face Death.

Ancient Crone,
Mother of wise endings,
I am at your crossroads.
A shadowy place of night,
Where I and my beloved must part.
But the darkness is full of your great and brilliant
stars.
And there is beauty to be seen, even in a parting of
ways.
Touch me, O Ancient Mother,
And carry me if needs be,
And in my sadness, I will gain great strength,
As I surrender to your immortal divinity.
Time moves forward,
And though the body of my Beloved will cease [or has
ceased],
[Her/His] spirit will live forever.

The petals fall from the rose,
And gently they touch ground.
The leaves also have fallen,
But a new seedling has already begun to arise.
[Her/His] life will not end.

[Her/His] ancient ancestry roamed the wild forests,
Hunted for food,
And lived by sunrise and sunset,

Knowing already of the magic and mystery,
Inherent in every day.
And this primordial mystery
Glowed from within [her/his] blessed eyes.

Place myrrh on the censer coal and light the black candle. Say:

Ancient Crone,
Gentle hand of death,
I call you forward and shall not fear you.

Light the white candle and say:

To the Eternal, within my own soul,
I call you to bring your light unto this parting.

Light the violet candle and say:

To my beloved,
I call the ancient wisdom of your soul unto this rite.

Move the black Crone candle forward until it stands between the white and the violet candle. Then, bring the white and violet candles slowly toward the black candle, until the three stand close together. Next, move the white and violet candles apart, away from the black candle, until they are as far apart as they can be, at opposite ends of your altar. Place a single blossom at the foot of the black candle, as an offering to the Crone. Cense the candles and your altar with fragrant smoke.

If your familiar has not yet died, be with her or him as much as you are able until the time comes. If he/she is gone, pray to his or her spirit. When the spirit has passed from the body of your pet, take the flowers used in this rite and scatter them in a wild natural setting.

An Honorable Farewell

Celebration at the transition of death

This ritual addresses the empty place that a friend or family member leaves when he or she dies. Their physical presence is gone from the earth. We honor them in a holy and respectful way, and in spirit they attend the celebration. Until they move on to the higher realms, they are close by us. For some, they remain close now and then throughout our lives, occasionally advising, reminding, and encouraging us, until we meet them on the other side after our own death. My maternal grandmother has continued to be a part of my life in this way

ITEMS NEEDED   Whiskey, port, or brandy (or juice), and a glass; votive candles in holders; flowers, food, and drink; and several important belongings of the desceased (these items should show the abilities and interests of the one who has died).

THE ALTAR   Arrange the belongings of the deceased around a chair, which will be kept vacant during the celebration. This empty chair invites the deceased to be a guest. This is the altar. Set out the food, drink, and flowers around the chair. Place candles on either side of the chair. All participants should bring flowers for the deceased, plus food and drink for a feast afterward.

TIMING AND INSTRUCTIONS   This rite is to be held approximately three days to a week after the loved one has parted. Music that the deceased was fond of should be played as everyone begins to arrive. (In addition, feel free to adapt the words of this rite to the person being mourned.)

BODY OF RITUAL   When everyone has arrived, stop the music and form a standing circle to the side of the altar.

The Circle

As mourners in the circle join hands, explain that the empty chair is the altar and makes a place for the deceased to attend the celebration. All participants should begin to hum, over which the following lines are spoken:

A participant says:

> *You are gone from this life.*
> *We miss you.*
> *There was a special place that you filled*
> *Which is now full of emptiness.*
> *You can never be replaced,*
> *For you were special and unique.*
>
> *Please forgive us our inadequacies.*
> *If we did not love you enough,*
> *Or in the right way.*
> *Please forgive us, if we misunderstood you at times*
> *Or did not listen to your heart.*
>
> *But hear us now,*
> *As we express our love*
> *And our appreciation for you.*
>
> *We know that your time here is done,*
> *And that we must let you go,*
> *But we will miss you*
> *And we sorrow at our loss.*

The Praises

A glass of whiskey, port, or brandy (or juice) is poured. The glass is passed around the circle. As the glass is received, praise of the deceased is given, or a positive personal incident is recounted. Then the glass is lifted as the participant says: *"To [deceased's name]!"* The participant takes a drink and the glass is passed to the next person who also gives the praise and the greeting, and so on, all around.

The Giving of Flowers

All begin the chant below (change gender as required). You can add a melody if you like.

> *Soon to the Higher Realms,*
> *Daughter, Soul, Sister, Friend,*
> *Love—love to thee.*

During the chant, each participant may go to the altar of the disceased to offer flowers and say any personal good-byes.

The Prayer of Farewell

One person reads a line at a time, and the other participants repeat it, as in a call-and-response:

> *[Name of deceased],*
> *Take now the high road*
> *Unto the Sacred Heavens.*
> *O spirit whom we love,*
> *Go as you will,*
> *Unto the beauty and glory*
> *Of that heavenly domain.*
> *Though we will miss you,*
> *Love and friendship will never be lost,*
> *And we will meet again one day,*
> *On the joyful road of Eternity*
> *Where the soul flies in freedom.*

It is with love
That we say farewell
To [name of deceased]
All say farewell.
So be it.
Blessed Be.

The Feast

Play the deceased's favorite music and share the food and drink everyone has brought.

7

Multifarious
Miscellany

Spiral of the Delphic Oracle

To obtain the answer to a question

This ritual requires the votary's ability to move into trance state. This is accomplished through deep focus, particularly in envisioning the Temple of Gaea, and in the descent of the spirals described below. It also requires the votary to suspend judgment as the words of the Oracle come forward. As you will become both votary and Oracle, there must be a sense of personal detachment during the process of receiving Gaea's words. In addition, the liturgy may be altered to denote the votary as Priest instead of Priestess.

ITEMS NEEDED   Incense of 5 parts powdered myrrh, 1 part dried mint, and 1/4 part ground cloves; a censer and censer coal; seven white votive candles in holders; bay leaves; offerings of bread, honey, and flowers; an image of a snake; a handful of Epsom salts or sea salt for a bath; a notebook or journal and a pen; enough small stones with which to circle your censer; a large bowl of water; and a prepared light meal to be eaten after the rite.

THE ALTAR   Place the censer in the center of the altar with the dish of mixed incense to the side. Arrange the stones around the censer. Place the seven candles in a wide circle around the censer. Inside the ring of candles, arrange a circle of bay leaves. Have the offerings, and the notebook and pen adjacent to the altar. Place the bowl of water on the floor to the side of the altar, in a place that is easily accessible to you while you are seated at the altar. Place all other items on the altar.

TIMING AND INSTRUCTIONS   The duration of this rite is one night, to to be held on the full moon or one night prior to the full moon, with activities the following morning. Refrain from sex for seven days prior to and including the day of the rite. During the day of the rite eat lightly of grains, nuts, fruits, and vegetables (unless health prohibits). Write your question in the notebook and place the notebook beside the altar with the page open to your question.

Make sure you are familiar with the entire rite; memorize the Trance Chant. You may want to add melody to it, or chant it on one note.

Before the rite take a bath to which you have added one handful of Epsom salts or sea salt. While in the bath, imagine the spiral that you will walk during the visioning part of the rite. Remember that when you are writing the words of the Oracle, you must not think or judge.

Dress simply in loose clothing. Light the censer coal a few minutes before the rite. If you have a tape or CD of slow, rhythmic drumming or other spiritual music, it would be good to play it at low volume throughout the rite.

BODY OF RITUAL   Place the incense on the coal. Cense the room by moving around the periphery in a clockwise direction, spiraling into the center. When you are in the center of the room, lift the censer up toward the ceiling and then down toward the floor. Return to the altar and set the censer down in the center. Be seated at your altar and say:

> *Delphi, ancient Temple of Gaea,*
> *Your beauty gleams white*
> *With noble columns and facades that are full of*
> *   splendor.*
> *Here your eternal spring flows softly beside the temple*
> *   wall.*

Branches of laurel bend and sway in the light breeze,
And the air is sweet with lavender and fennel.
Home of the Pythia, Daughter of Gaea,
Serpent priestess of the Great Mother.
Chaste mouth of the oracle.
Here, rock and stone are alive with the words of the
    First Mother.

Gaea! Venerable Womb of Creation,
Your power seeps up from the earth
Like fragrant smoke.
It rises through ancient stony caverns,
Potent as dark aged wine.

I have prepared to approach the Oracle.
Here are my offerings of bread, honey, and flowers.

Place the offerings on the altar. Then, in your inner vision, see
the eternal spring of Delphi flow out of the craggy rocks. See the
water sparkle and shine in the sunlight. Hear the sounds of the
water flowing. Hear the voices of the other priestesses saying,
"*Take from the eternal spring!*" You reply:

Sacred water,
You are a part of the body of the Great Mother.
Deep oceans, silver rains,
Bright rivers, and sparkling streams,
All born from Gaea.

Here her spring rushes forward
And fills the stony basin.
Drinking of her waters,
I drink of the First Mother.

Dip your cupped hands into the bowl; take water from it, and
drink from her ancient spring. Then dip your hands into the

bowl and sprinkle her waters on your body. Anoint your face, arms, and so on, saying, *"Blessed by the waters of Gaea."*

Envision walking up the marble steps to her temple, through the columns, and into the portico. You walk through the temple into the Room of the Oracle. You see a tripod chair. Around the bottom of the chair is a large snake. Next to the chair is an altar. The snake raises its head to greet you. Approach the altar, which has a ring of candles on it.

Light a candle toward the back of the circle of candles on your altar and say:

> *Gaea, Mother of Earth,*
> *Rich, wise, and primeval in power,*
> *I have entered the chamber of Delphi*
> *As your votary and priestess.*

Bow your head to the ancient Earth Mother. Place more incense on the censer coal. See the smoke rise up. Close your eyes and call Gaea to you. Light each candle on the altar, always moving to the right of the one that is already lit. Say one phrase for each candle:

> *"Gaea, your power rises from deep Earth."*
> *"Your wisdom ascends."*
> *"True words seek a voice."*
> *"Your fire sings."*
> *"I am prepared for your wisdom."*

Feel Gaea enter the room as you light the last candle. See yourself in the Temple of the Oracle seated on the tripod. Say:

> *I am the Oracle, the Priestess Pythia.*
> *And I shall become the voice of Gaea.*

Sprinkle more incense on the coal and say:

> *Wise and most honored Mother.*
> *You are the heart of the Earth.*

Heart of fire, sing to me . . .
Smoke rise, sing to me . . .
The power of the Oracle rushes like the wind.

Say the Trance Chant until you are in trance state:

Smoke rise and fire sing,
Gaea come, your power bring.

Visioning

Move deeply inward, then down, down, into the Earth. Begin to see that you are walking the outside edge of a spiral. The spiral path spins inward and downward. You are walking inward toward its center, descending deeply into the Earth. Walk the spiral. Descend into the heart of the Earth.

Becoming One With Gaea

When you arrive at the center of the spiral, the center of the Earth, immerse yourself in her fire; float in her fire. You are in the heart of the Earth, inside of her. You become one with her body. Your heart is her heart. You are filled with her fiery passion, and you know all. Say:

My body, her body,
My heart, her heart.
My mind, her mind.
Here is her knowledge and her fire.
Her passion flows through me.
Her wisdom is known to me.
I speak for her.
The Oracle is ready.
Present your questions.

Asking the Oracle

Take up your paper and read the question you've written. Turn to a fresh page and pick up the pen. Ask your question aloud, then listen—and write. Let the words flow until there are none left.

Releasing the Energies

When you are done, set your work down. Sprinkle incense on the coal. Place your hands on your heart and bow to Gaea. Dip your hands in the bowl of water and run them over your face. Stand up and take a deep breath and exhale, bending over at the waist. Let your arms and head dangle down, releasing the energies. Go into your kitchen and eat a light meal, then bathe or shower. Extinguish the candles with a snuffer or inverted cup, saying, *"Praises to Gaea."*

The Following Morning

Relight the candles and make tea, using some of the honey from the altar. Drink your tea as you review the words of the Oracle. Look for both overt and underlying themes and ideas, and write your interpretations on a new page. When you are done, place the flowers and cakes outside in a wild place in nature. Place your hands on the Earth and thank Gaea.

THE RITE OF THE NON-RITUAL

For joy in the moment

The idea of the non-ritual is to pause in the pursuit of your goals in order to enjoy the beauty of the moment. It's an experience for you alone, free from the constraints of time and responsibility; a kind of a one-day vacation. You create it by placing yourself in a beautiful environment and bringing an attitude of inner quiet and observation to your experience. One thing that helps in doing this is not to talk or to participate in as little conversation as possible. Many years ago I injured my vocal cords and had to spend a week without making a sound. I found that when you accept the silence, it allows your other senses to become more alert. I communicated with people by writing. If you can, try silence for one day; prepare to observe, listen, see, and feel.

Choose a place that you consider to have great beauty. It can be a seashore or marina, or a spot in the countryside. It can be a museum, a building of wonderful architectural proportions, a garden, or any other place that you appreciate as beautiful. Choose a day in which you have no other responsibilities.

Wear something in which you feel comfortable. Take lunch with you, or dine out. The plan is for you to be a quiet observer. Sometimes we can be in a place of great beauty but we do not see or feel it because the mind is busy with problems, incomplete goals, or conversation. This ritual is useful to quiet a stressed or busy mind, or to use simply to enjoy being alive.

My recent non-ritual day was spent at a local marina. I had discovered a need to be near the sea. I listened to the seagulls and watched their beautiful movements closely. I was awed by their perfect form. Sailboats were going to and fro with their lovely white sails. I paused at the railing several times to look out at the sea. I walked, feeling the breeze through my hair and on my arms. I felt completely carefree. I had nothing else to do in all the world but to be right where I was.

The air smelled of the sea, delightfully fresh and invigorating. I took deep breaths full of it. It was slightly cloudy and the water was gray, but where the sun shone on the sea it was like a thousand diamonds flickering on the surface. I was quiet inside as I made these observations. These were beautiful moments of just being.

I had a bowl of great clam chowder, and purchased some inexpensive little seashells to take home with me to remember my day. It was a very simple day, full of the joy of being in the moment. Try it!

EVENING RITUAL FOR THE GREAT MOTHER

To offer thanks and appreciation

In this rite we give our thanks to the Great Mother for the life that we have been given. This is meant be done with a group or can be adapted for the solitary worshiper. The spirit is lifted by giving thanks for life, and for all that has been birthed by the Great Creatress.

ITEMS NEEDED   Image or statue of the Goddess; three white taper candles; bread, wine, and a cup for each participant; flowers in a vase; a censer and sandalwood stick incense.

THE ALTAR   Set up your altar with the above items, placing the three candles in a row facing you. Open a window near the altar so that some of the incense smoke will drift outside.

TIMING AND INSTRUCTIONS   This rite may be held at any time of the lunar cycle, and should be done before a meal. The stanzas marked "Cleric" may be shared among the participants. To change the rite so that it can be performed by one person, substitute *I* for *we*. Dinner should follow the ritual.

BODY OF RITUAL   The cleric says:

> *To the Great Mother*
> *We offer honor, praises, and thanksgiving*
> *For all that has been created.*
>
> *For the rising and the setting Sun,*
> *For the ever-changing luminous Moon,*
> *For the brilliant and distant stars,*
> *And for the mysteries of nature.*
> *For these, we give thanks.*

The cleric lights the first candle. All say *"Great is the Mother of Life."*

The cleric says:

> *For kindness among friends and strangers,*
> *For our abilities and our vocations,*
> *And for the richness of the Earth,*
> *We give our thanks.*

The cleric lights the second candle. All say, *"Great is the Mother of Life."*

The cleric says:

> *For eyes that see the divinity of life,*
> *For the heart that lives in compassion,*
> *And for wisdom by which we appreciate*
> *All that has been given,*
> *We give our thanks.*

The cleric lights the third candle. All say, *"Great is the Mother of Life."*

The cleric picks up the bread and says, *"By her body are we sustained."* All participants repeat the cleric's words, *"By her body are we sustained."*

The cleric breaks the bread and passes it around, saying, *"From her fields comes the bounty of the Earth."*

All repeat, *"From her fields comes the bounty of the Earth."*

The cleric says, *"All eat in her honor."*

All participants partake of the bread.

The cleric picks up the wine and says, *"By her fruitful body are we sustained."*

The participants repeat, *"By her fruitful body are we sustained."*

The cleric pours wine into the cups and says, *"From vine and tree comes the fruit of the Earth."*

All repeat, *"From vine and tree comes the fruit of the Earth."*
The cleric says, *"All drink in her honor."* The cups are passed out and all drink.

The cleric lights incense, raises the censer, and says:

> *May our praises and thanksgiving rise,*
> *Unto the heart of the Great Mother!*
> *Blessed Be.*

The participants say, *"Blessed Be!"*
Retire to dinner while the candles burn down.

ONE HUNDRED NAMES
OF THE GREAT MOTHER

A Goddess meditation

This rite was inspired by the Hindu practice of reciting Goddess names and powers one after the other as a long form of meditation.

ITEMS NEEDED   One white candle in holder; flowers; censer; and incense.

THE ALTAR   Place the above items on the altar.

TIMING AND INSTRUCTIONS   This rite can be done any time of the lunar cycle. It can be used in its entirety, or separate stanzas can be used as individual morning and evening meditations. There are fourteen stanzas. As a week-long meditation, each morning light a candle and say two stanzas. It can also be done in entirety as a ritual with several people per stanza, alternating stanzas in groups, and building energy as you go.

Light the candle and incense. Gaze into the flame, and begin.

First Stanza

Many are the names of the Great Mother . . .
Amphitrite, beautiful Sea Mother, bless the world
with your many riches.
Aphrodite, Goddess of Love, bring love's joy and
pleasure into my life.
Ariadne, High Fruitful One, bless me with your great
bounty.
Arianrhod, Goddess of the Stars, grant me your
all-seeing wisdom.

Artemis, Mother of All Creatures, nurture me with
   your power.
Athena, holy virgin, bless me with strength and
   knowledge.
Aurora, Goddess of the Dawn, bless the world with
   bright eternal hope.
All honor to the Great Mother.

Second Stanza

Many are the names of the Great Mother . . .
Badba, bless me with all things fair from within your
   deep cauldron.
Blodeuwedd, Flowering Spring Maiden, bless my life
   with beauty.
Brigid, bring your light, your magic, and the power to
   heal, to me.
Callisto, fair queen, bless me with your great strength
   and power.
Ceres, Great Earth Mother, bless me with a
   prosperous life.
Cerridwen, Lady of the Cauldron of Inspiration, bring
   me bright thought.
Chthonia, Underworld Goddess, make me wise and
   fearless.
All honor to the Great Mother.

Third Stanza

Many are the names of the Great Mother . . .
Clotho, spin into my fate, health, happiness, and
   contentment.

*Coventina, Goddess of Sparkling Streams, bring me
    laughter.*

*Cyrene, bring the power of transforming magic into
    the world.*

Danu, Earth Mother, bring me strength and wisdom.

*Dea Mater, Earth Mother, teach me of your
    mysteries.*

*Diana, Queen of Heaven and Mother of Creatures,
    bless me with love.*

Durga, bring me the strength that leads to victory.

All honor to the Great Mother.

Fourth Stanza

Many are the names of the Great Mother . . .

Eostre, Goddess of Spring, bring me health and joy.

*Eide, Goddess of Feminine Wisdom, bless me with
    bright intelligence.*

*Eos, fair Mother Dawn, let happiness be born in my
    heart.*

*Eurynome, Universal Mother, let me understand all
    people.*

*Flora, Goddess of Spring, may my life flourish in
    beauty.*

*Fortuna, Goddess of Good Fortune, bless me through
    the day and night.*

Freya, Beautiful Mother, bless me with loving care.

All honor to the Great Mother.

Fifth Stanza

Many are the names of the Great Mother . . .

*Gaea, Divine Earth, upon your body I live. Bless me,
    great one.*

*Galatea, White Moon Mother, bless me with plenty
    and prosperity.*
Ganges, Mother of Rivers, cleanse and purify my soul.
Gauri, Golden One, Lady of Fair Bliss, comfort me.
*Hathor, Queen of Heaven, bless me with thy eternal
    wisdom and beauty.*
Hebe, let me taste the ambrosia of my immortal soul.
*Hecate, lunar Goddess of Light and Dark, teach me
    your magic.*
All honor to the Great Mother.

Sixth Stanza

Many are the names of the Great Mother . . .
Hestia, Goddess of the Hearth Flame, bless my home.
*Hsi Wang Mu, Royal Mother of Paradise, let me
    know your beauty.*
Hygea, Goddess of Health, grant me a strong body.
*Ilithyia, divine midwife, may all children grow in
    health.*
*Inanna, fertile mother, daily renew my spirit with
    love.*
*Iris, bridge between Earth and Heaven, let your
    rainbow colors bless me.*
*Isis, giver of life, bless me with your magic and great
    power.*
All honor to the Great Mother.

Seventh Stanza

Many are the names of the Great Mother . . .
Juno, Great Maternal Being, care for and protect me.

Kali-Ma, Dark Mother, bring me the wisdom of right endings.

Kilya, Bright Mother Moon, teach me of life's divine patterns.

Kore, blessed Spring Maiden, sing your song of joy unto my heart.

Kwan Yin, tender-hearted Mother of All, let me live with your compassion.

Lakshmi, sovereign Goddess of Bounty and Prosperity, bless all people.

Lilith, First Mother, bless my life with fertile possibilities.

All honor to the Great Mother.

Eighth Stanza

Many are the names of the Great Mother . . .

Lucina, Mother of Light, let me carry your light into dark places.

Luna, Mother Moon, bless me with your iridescent magic.

Maat, Lady of Justice, bring all things to a balance within my life.

Maia, Mother of Wisdom and magic, let me hear your song.

Mari, Sea Mother, may I honor the power of the deep ocean.

Mary, Queen of Heaven, bless me with a compassionate heart.

Mera, Mother of the Nile Waters, bless our Earth.

All honor to the Great Mother.

Ninth Stanza

Many are the names of the Great Mother . . .
Metis, Mother of Athena, grant blessings to all of
  deep wisdom.
Nanshe, ancient Mother of Deep Waters, help me
  understand my dreams.
Nimue, Goddess of the Moon, enchant my life with
  beauty.
Ninhursag, Ancient Earth Mother, grant me a life of
  contentment.
Nuit, Goddess of the Starry Night Sky, lend me light
  when I have need.
Nu-kua, Goddess of Marriage, bring bliss unto all
  sacred lovers.
Om, Mother of Mantras, bless me.
All honor to the Great Mother.

Tenth Stanza

Many are the names of the Great Mother . . .
Panacea, all-healing daughter of Rhea, bless me with
  health.
PanGaea, Universal Mother, bring the world into
  peace and accord.
Parvati, virgin daughter of the Heavens, bless my life
  with beauty.
Pasiphae, Lady Who Shines for All, send your light
  into the darkest heart.
Persephone, Queen of the Underworld, set me a place
  in fair elysium.

Pomona, Fruitful Mother, send your abundant
  goodwill into my life.
Prakriti, Goddess of Nature, may I see the divinity in
  Earth, sea, and sky.
All honor to the Great Mother.

Eleventh Stanza

Many are the names of the Great Mother . . .
Radha, Goddess of Loving Desire, through your power
  may I know bliss.
Rangi, Sky Mother, bless me with far-ranging vision.
Rhea, Mother of Life, Death, and Rebirth, grant me
  a full life well lived.
Samjna, Goddess of Signs and Letters, let all I write
  bring understanding.
Saraswati, flowing one, Goddess of Wisdom and All
  the Arts, bless me.
Selene, Lady of the Moon, bless me with bright
  intuition.
Shakti, Goddess of Cosmic Energy, I bow to you.
All honor to the Great Mother.

Twelfth Stanza

Many are the names of the Great Mother . . .
Shashti, protectress of children, bless us, for we are all
  your children.
Shekina, may I unite with thy light and glory.
Siduri Sabitu, enlighten me with the wine of
  paradise.
Sophia, send your holy dove to bring peace unto my
  soul.

*Stella Maris, star of the sea, guide me in my life's
    journey.
Sulis, eye of the sun, send your rays of light unto all.
Sybil, Great Mother, bring the wisdom of the Oracle
    unto my life.
All honor to the Great Mother.*

Thirteenth Stanza

*Many are the names of the Great Mother . . .
Tara, Goddess of the Living Earth, revered in all the
    arts, bless me.
Taueret, bless all women with ease at childbirth.
Tefnut, Goddess of Rain and of sparkling dew, refresh
    my soul.
Terra, deep breasted Earth, ancient one, I bow to you.
Thalia, creatress of music, beautiful one, may my
    spirit sing.
Themis, divine Goddess of Knowledge and Magic,
    grant me wisdom.
Tiamat, Creatress Who Gave Birth to the Universe,
    bless my spirit.
Tyche, Mother of Fortune and Destiny, bless my life
    with goodness.
All honor to the Great Mother.*

Fourteenth Stanza

*Many are the names of the Great Mother . . .
Uma, Mother Love, surround me with sweet caresses.
Urd, Fountain of Wisdom, may I awake to your
    perfect knowledge.*

Ushas, Goddess of the Dawn, awake my heart with joy.

Vach, Creatress of the Om, of all sound and speech, bless my words.

Venus, evening star and Goddess of Love, bring me the light of pure loving.

Vesta, Goddess of Bright Temple Fires, bless my prayer.

Yin, feminine force of the white tiger, grant me health.

Zoe, Mother of All Living Things, I praise the perfect miracle that is life.

All honor to the Great Mother.

8

The Goddess
and the God

INVOKING THE GODDESS AND THE GOD

Calling them into your circle

Either of these invocations can be added singly to any ritual you feel would be appropriate, or they can be used together as they are presented. They can also form a part of Sabbat celebrations.

ITEMS NEEDED   Two candles in holders and decorations from nature (see below).

THE ALTAR   Surround the candles by what is seasonally appropriate for your area at the time such as greenery, flowers, fruit, pine branches and cones, autumn leaves, grain, bare winter branches, and so on.

TIMING AND INSTRUCTIONS   This rite can be held at any time in the lunar cycle.

Invoking the Goddess

Say:

> *Divine Mother of all the living,*
> *Of the shining stars within the dark womb of night,*
> *And of all the green and wondrous Earth,*
> *I bow to you.*
>
> *The wheel turns*
> *As you weave the fabric of mortal life.*

Spring, summer, winter, and fall;
You are Mistress of all Seasons.

Creatress of the animals:
Of all those winged creatures who fly,
Of those living in watery domains,
And of those who move across the vast Earth,
O you are Mother of them all.

To you who have created the human form,
And endowed flesh with unending spirit,
To you who have given so much,
I give thanks, and bow to your mystery.

O Lady of Deep Wisdom,
You are the fullness and sweetness of life.
Triple Queen of the sacred and iridescent moon . . .
Joyful, powerful, and wise,
You are truth and eternal beauty.
O Lady of Life,
Thou art the living Goddess.
Bless me, make me one and whole.

Light a candle, saying *"Hail to the Lady of Life!"*

Invoking the God

Say:

Divine Father of all the living,
Of the sun, who makes fruitful our beloved earth,
Of lightning shining in the heavens,
And of the blessed rains,
I bow to you.

In deep forests, you are Lord of the Animals.
O player of pipes in the greenwood,
You bring music to the Dance of Life.
You are filled with life, and the joy of being.

At spring's renewal,
You dance with the maiden Goddess
Bringing new life to Earth.
In summer, to her you are wed.
Autumn's rich harvest follows,
And when it is done you journey back to her dark
    womb,
Whence you are eternally reborn.
When the cold of winter arrives,
You are born again from the Great Mother,
As the besplendored light of the waxing sun.

This is your Sacred Dance,
And as you dance the wheel turns,
And the seasons move through time.
For you are the key to life, death, and rebirth.
O Lord of Life, thou art the living God.
Bless me, make me one and whole.

Light the second candle, saying, *"Hail to the Lord of Life!"*

DRAWING DOWN THE MOON

Rite for the Goddess at the full moon

For the priestess, this ritual heightens your awareness of the full moon. It may form a part of your Sabbat celebration if your Sabbat falls on or near a full moon, or it may be added to any other ritual that takes place on the full moon. It may also be used as a rite of personal visioning-magic, with the visualization of a desired goal performed at the end of the rite. Or, it can simply be used as a way to experience and honor Mother Moon. Another option is to follow it with the rite for Pan, and then the rite of the Sacred Marriage.

ITEMS NEEDED   Chalice of wine or juice; incense of choice; censer; six white votive candles in holders; a vase of white flowers; and a head wreath of white flowers or a silver jeweled crown (a sewn ring of silver trim with sewn-on stones).

THE ALTAR   Arrange the six votive candles in a circle. Place the rest of the items on the altar. This rite is arranged for an outdoor altar and may be adapted for indoor use.

TIMING AND INSTRUCTIONS   Ideally, this rite is to be done on the night of the full moon; it my also be done the day before or the day after. Note that at certain months of the year the full moon may still be below the horizon at the time you want to do your rite. Consult an ephemeris for the full moon's rising time on a specific night.

Stand at your altar, and say:

> *Silver disc of the moon,*
> *Glowing pearl of the nighttime sky,*
> *Fill me with your radiant and iridescent light.*

O Lady of the Moon,
With mystery and grace
Your shining light flows out into the ethers.
In magic, you pour your silver wine
Into the black chalice of the heavens.

Luna, Artemis, Diana . . . adorned with luminous stars,
You are the Empress of the Skies.
You are the brilliant dawn, filled with all human hope.
You are sweet flowers touched with morning dew.
For the gifts of dark night, move across the spinning
    Earth,
To freshen the awakening land.

Light the incense and let the fragrant smoke rise. Hold the censer up and say:

O Mother of all, I honor and praise you.
Come, bring me the magic of the night
And of the silver moon.
Fill me with your ancient power.

Place the censer down. Light the ring of six white candles, saying the following Goddess names for each candle:

Hail, Luna!
Hail, Diana!
Hail, Albion!
Hail, Selene!
Hail, Artemis!
Hail, Isis!

Raise your glass of wine to her. Pour a small libation of wine onto the ground (if you're indoors, use a libation bowl), and say, *"Praises to the Mistress of the Moon!"*

Pour a second libation of wine, saying, *"To the Goddess of Earth and heaven!"*

Pour a third libation, saying: *"To the Lady of the dark and glittering sky!"*

Take a sip of wine, and set the chalice down. Set the wreath of white flowers or the silver jeweled crown upon your head and raise your arms up to her. Say:

> *Lady of power and magic!*
> *Come, descend upon this,*
> *The body of thy votary and priestess here.*

Raise your arms toward her and with your breath, draw her light and power down into your body. Feel the magic of her irridescent light. Pause in this state, drawing her down for as long as you wish. Let your body fill with her power. Then say:

> *I am the Lady of the Moon*
> *Amidst the dark skies.*
> *I am Luna and bright Diana.*
> *In shining beauty,*
> *I am Albion and Selene.*
> *In power and magic,*
> *I am Artemis . . . and I am Isis.*

Place the chalice in the center of the ring of candles. You may let the candles burn down completely.

You may end your rite here, or you may continue with any other rite that might benefit from the power of Drawing Down the Moon. Or use your powers to envision a desire or goal you seek. Fill that vision with the light and power of the Lady of the Full Moon. When you are done, release and ground the energies by letting all excess energies flow into the earth below you. At the end of the rite remove the crown, divesting yourself of deity.

An option is to perform this rite and then have a partner follow it with the Rite to Invoke Pan. This may be followed by the Sacred Marriage.

Rite to Invoke Pan

For the God

This rite heightens the priest's awareness of the God of Nature. It brings the power of Pan, the Greek God of Woodlands and Forests, into the spirit of the votary. Vested with the divinity of Pan, you will feel his power, hear his song, and know his Sacred Dance. This rite may be done with a partner in concert with Drawing Down the Moon.

Items Needed   Incense and censer; six green votive candles in holders; a chalice of wine or juice; and a head wreath of green leaves.

The Altar   Arrange candles in a circle on the altar. Place censer, incense, chalice of wine or juice, and the crown of green leaves on the altar.

Timing and Instructions   This ritual is ideally done on the night of the full moon, or may be done the day before or the day after. Note that at certain months of the year, the full moon may still be below the horizon at the time you want to do your rite. Consult an ephemeris for the full moon's rising time on a specific night.

Body of Ritual   Stand at your altar and say:

> *Great Pan,*
> *Your forest is all light and shadow,*
> *Rustling with scents of pine, and oak.*
> *With cool breezes and mysterious melodies,*
> *You play your pipes under the green canopy.*
>
> *Horned and hooved leader of the dance,*
> *Upon your pipes you play sweet sounds,*
> *Sometimes soft, sometimes boisterous.*

Great are the songs of your sacred spirit,
For at your hand is all the wide chorus of nature.

Your songs descend into shaded glens,
And run with deer across wide meadows.
Nature rejoices in your presence,
As you play your magic
Of silver light and green shadow.

Light the incense and let the fragrant smoke rise. Hold the censer out and say:

Lord of woodlands and wild creatures,
Mischievous, subtle, and bright with laughter,
O God of green Arcadia,
Who brings joy, passion, and magic to the dance
*   of life,*
Come and attend me in this rite.

Place the censer down. Light the ring of six green votive candles, saying the following God names for each candle:

Hail, Pan!
Hail, Faunus!
Hail, Dionysus!
Hail, Bacchus!
Hail, Liber!
Hail, Osiris!

Raise your glass of wine to him. Pour a small libation onto the ground (if indoors, use a libation bowl) and say, *"Praises to the God of Nature!"*

Pour a second libation of wine onto the ground saying, *"To the Great Lord of the Forests!"*

Pour a third libation saying, *"To the horned and hooved leader of the Dance!"*

Take a sip of wine, and set the chalice down. Set the wreath of green leaves upon your head. Raise your arms outward to him and say:

> *Lord of power and magic!*
> *Come, descend upon this,*
> *The body of thy votary and priest.*

With arms raised out to all of nature, to all that grows, and to the world of the animals, with a breath, draw his power into your body. Feel his magic. Pause in this state, drawing him in for as long as you wish. Then say:

> *I am the Lord of Nature,*
> *God of the wild woodlands.*
> *I am Pan and Faunus,*
> *Mine is the Sacred Dance of the deep forest.*
> *I am Dionysus and Bacchus,*
> *The ever-present miracle and song of life.*
> *In power and magic,*
> *I am Liber . . . and I am Osiris.*

Place the chalice in the center of the ring of candles. Let the candles burn down completely.

This may end your rite, or use your powers to envision a desire, or goal you seek. Fill that vision with the light and power of the Lord of Nature. When you are done, release and ground the energies by letting excess energies flow into the earth. You may use this rite by itself or before beginning another rite. At the end of the rite, remove the crown, divesting yourself of deity.

If a partner has performed Drawing Down the Moon, you may follow this rite with the Sacred Marriage.

THE SACRED MARRIAGE

Ritual union of the God and Goddess

This rite is designed to follow the rites to invoke Pan and Drawing Down the Moon. At this point, the priestess and priest are vested with the power of the Goddess and God. The Sacred Marriage is the union of these two aspects of divinity, male and female, with body and soul. Let the love that enters, move beyond personality, and come from the universal force beyond body and mind.

ITEMS NEEDED   Sandalwood stick incense; One foot each of green ribbon and white ribbon; and fragrant oil of your choice, to be used on both the priestess and priest.

THE ALTAR   Green and white candles are already lit on the altars for Drawing Down the Moon and the Rite to Invoke Pan. You will also need space in which to dance, and a comfortable place to recline.

TIMING AND INSTRUCTIONS   This rite is ideally done on the night of the full moon, but it may also be done the day before or the day after. Note that at certain months of the year, the full moon may still be below the horizon at the time you want to do your rite. Consult an ephemeris for the time of the full moon's rising on a specific night.

BODY OF RITUAL   Light the sandalwood incense. The priestess and priest should stand several feet apart and say together:

> *With love and trust,*
> *Shall we attend the Sacred Marriage.*
> *Now shall the God and Goddess*
> *Complete the Dance.*

The priest says to the priestess:

>*Lady of the Moon,*
>*Goddess of all things,*
>*Draw near, and join me in the Dance.*
>*May the beauty and power of the deep forest*
>*Surround you with passion.*
>*Here is the perfect gift of the God.*

The priestess says to the priest:

>*Lord of the forests and of wild, untamed nature,*
>*Draw near me, and drink of my powers,*
>*As I shall drink of thine,*
>*For I am the moon's luminous joy,*
>*And the night's deepest mystery.*
>*Here is the perfect gift of the Goddess.*

The priest takes one step closer to the priestess and says:

>*The white hawthorn blooms,*
>*The wild rose is red and fragrant,*
>*The elderberry, dark and sweet,*
>*All created in perfect beauty.*
>*Just as you, who are perfect beauty.*
>*Just as you.*

The priestess takes one step closer to the priest and says:

>*Deer run free in the forest,*
>*Birds soar across the skies,*
>*Untamed nature holds the key to the mystery.*
>*The symphony of life plays its divine melody*
>*And I am drawn to you.*
>*Come, rest in my moonlit cave upon soft green rushes*
>*Where I will sing joy unto thy soul.*

The priest kisses the priestess on her chest above her heart, on the palms of her hands, and on her forehead, then says, *"Come, attend my fire-lit festival."*

The priestess kisses a spot on the priest's chest above his heart, on the palms of his hands, and on his forehead, then says, *"Yes, I come to the Dance."*

The priest ties the green ribbon around the priestess's wrist. He anoints her heart with fragrant oil, saying, *"Great Lady of the Moon, honor me with your love."*

The priestess ties the white ribbon around the priest's wrist. She anoints his heart with fragrant oil, saying: *"Great Lord of the Forests, honor me with your love."*

The priest addresses the priestess saying, *"Luna . . . Selene . . . Isis . . ."*

The priestess addresses the priest saying, *"Dionysus . . . Osiris . . . Pan . . ."*

They say together:

> *We are the very forces of life and nature,*
> *Who enter into the Sacred Dance.*

The God and Goddess unite . . .

The Closing

When their "dance" has ended, the priestess says to the priest, *"Praises to the God, Lord of Life."*

The priest says to the priestess, *"Praises to the Goddess, Mother of Life."*

Wear the ribbons for twenty-four hours and remember.

9

The Celtic
Tree-Calendar
Alphabet

T he Celtic tree-calendar alphabet included a system that both named the months and provided knowledge of Druidic magical tree lore. Each Celtic month was assigned a tree-name and an ogham. The thirteen tree-months per year are Birch, Rowan, Alder, Willow, Ash, Hawthorn, Oak, Holly, Hazel, Vine, Ivy, Reed, and Elder. While these thirteen trees related to consonants, there were also additional tree-letters that related to vowels.

A solar year includes thirteen lunar months plus some additional days. Since one year is a count of the days the Earth takes to go around the Sun, the method of using thirteen moons to count one year was not exactly accurate. The Druids developed a system by which they would occasionally add an intercalculary month to their year. When a fourteenth month was added, it was done just after the Winter Solstice. This extra month of intercalculary days was assigned a fourteenth tree, the Silver Fir.

The Thirteen Tree-Months and Their Correspondences

The tree names, corresponding letters, oghams, and months listed on the next page are traditional. Affirmative statements accompany them. They are an adaptation of the Celtic "Song of the Amergin," a poem of Druidic tree lore. The affirmations remain true to the essence and traditional powers of the trees. They are used in the ritual Song of the Sacred Grove on page 169.

Tree	Poetic Affirmation	Ogham	Month
Birch	I am the light of every dawn.	Beth	12/25/ to 1/21
Rowan	I am the magic between the worlds.	Luis	1/22 to 2/18
Alder	I am the fire in darkest night.	Fearn	2/19 to 3/17
Willow	I am the magic of the changing moon.	Saille	3/18 to 4/14
Ash	I am the union of Earth and Sky.	Nion	4/15 to 5/12
Hawthorn	I am the purity of the white Mayblossom.	Huath	5/13 to 6/9
Oak	I am the door to every hope.	Duir	6/10 to 7/7
Holly	I am the battle won without blood.	Tinne	7/8 to 8/4
Hazel	I am the key to the waters of life.	Coll	8/5 to 9/1
Vine	I am the wisdom of unsung truth.	Muin	9/2 to 9/29
Ivy	I am the spiral of whirling time.	Gort	9/30 to 10/27
Reed	I am the arrow that finds its mark.	Ngetal	10/28 to 11/24
Elder	I am the cauldron, empty yet full.	Ruis	11/25 to 12/22

Birch: Purity, Overcoming, and New Beginnings

The Birch is sometimes called the Silver or White Birch. It has slender graceful branches, and its bark peels away in layers. Easy to see, it stands out from other forest growth, its green leaves contrasting beautifully with its whiteness. Birch is the first tree to put out new leaves after winter. Sometimes its little pale green flowers bloom even before its leaves appear. The Birch rod or broom drives away any negative energies from the old year, and prepares the way for the new year. The Celtic letter Beth and the letter B, are the letter names for Birch.

Rowan: Magical Powers, Insight, and Protection

The Rowan tree with its fernlike leaves is sometimes called Quickbeam, Quicken, or Mountain Ash. Its red berries have a dimple opposite the stem, which resembles a five-pointed star.

Rowan was considered holy and was set over doorways to keep evil away. It was also used in witches' charms to protect against lightning and enchantments. The Sabbat of Imbolg takes place during the Celtic tree-month of Rowan. The Celtic letter Luis and the letter L are the letter names for Rowan.

Alder: Fiery Strength, Steadfast Power, and Determination

The Alder resists decay; its oily wood was used for building foundations. The wood is white, but when it is cut its sap runs red. The bark was used for a red dye, and because of this, and the Alder's resistance to water, it was thought to have a fiery energy. Its leaves were used for green dye. Spring Equinox takes place during the Celtic tree-month of Alder. The Celtic letter Fearn and the letter F are the letter names for Alder.

Willow: Wisdom, Magic, Intuition, and Flexibility

The Willow has soft white wood and is associated with the Moon and the element water. Willow was often used for divining rods to find water. Its branches are flexible and from its name come the words *wicker*, *Wicca*, and *witch*. *Wiccar* was the witch's wisdom, and the ability to enchant and make magic. In the traditional witch's broom used to sweep clear the circle, Willow was used to bind the Ash stake to the broom. Willow was also used to make baskets, and its bark is a remedy for pain. Beltane takes place during the Celtic tree-month of Willow. The Celtic letter Saille and the letter S are the letter names for Willow.

Ash: Union of Earth and Spirit, of Inner and Outer Worlds, and the Guardian of Peace

The Ash has silver-gray bark and a very strong root system that moves deeply into the Earth. Its branches open wide to the heavens. Ash was used for oars, cart wheels, spears, and broom handles. The Ash tree-month is the month of melting snows and floods, and the time of winds and sea voyages. The Celtic letter Nion and the letter N are the letter names for Ash.

Hawthorn: Beauty, Purity, Fairy Magic, and Fertility

The Hawthorn is sometimes called Mayblossom, Haw-tree, or Thornapple. It bears a pleasant-scented white five-petaled flower, and a small dark red fruit called a haw. Hawthorn flowers were used in May weddings, and represent the purity and beauty of spring. Its beautiful fragrant flowering branches were said to be loved by fairies. it is also said to represent both chastity (white flowers), and fertility (red fruit). Hawthorn is often cut into a garden hedge to surround the garden with protection. The Celtic letter Huath and the letter H are the letter names for Hawthorn.

Oak: Strength, Endurance, Spiritual Guidance, and Balance

The Oak tree grows slowly, but its wood is strong and hard. It survives fire and lightning, and though burned, it bears new leaves and new growth. Oak is used for doors, and so its name came to mean *the door*. Considered a door to spiritual wisdom and guidance, the Oak was especially sacred to the Druids. The word *Druid* is related to the word *Duir*, and signifies those priests and priestesses who are a part of the cult of the Oak-King. At one time the ancient Oak forests made a great canopy across vast stretches of Europe. Its acorns were a source of food, and its strength a source of spiritual inspiration. The roots of the Oak extend deeply into the Earth and its branches rise high, and so somewhat like the Ash, it is a symbol for balance between earth and heaven. Summer Solstice takes place during the Celtic tree-month of Oak. The Celtic letter Duir and the letter D are the letter names for Oak.

Holly: Victory, Success, and Protection

The leaves of the Holly, Holly-Oak, or Holm-Oak are green throughout the year, even in winter. The flowers of the Holly-Oak produce a red dye, and so it was sometimes called the Bloody Oak. The Sabbat of Lughnasad takes place during the Celtic tree-month of Holly. A tree of protection, Holly was said to guard against evil spirits and intruders. Just as Holly follows the Oak of midsummer, this was the tree of the heir to the Celtic Oak-King. The Celtic letter Tinne and the letter T are the letter names for Holly and the sign of the Tanist, the Celtic King's successor. He carried a spear with a barbed point shaped like the letter Tinne.

Hazel: Spiritual Nourishment, Divination, and Knowledge

The Hazel is a small nut-bearing tree whose fruit ripens between August and September. This tree was of great importance not only for its food-bearing qualities, but for its pliant branches, which were used to divine sources of water. The Hazel tree was considered particularly sacred, and was never cut down for building or for any other purpose. The Celtic letter Coll and the letter C are the letter names for Hazel.

Vine: An Interweaving of the Physical and Spiritual Worlds

Wine, made from the fruit of the Vine, was the drink of poets, bards, and diviners. The Vine does not represent drunkenness, however, but a letting go of the logical and allowing the mystical to enter. In addition, the Vine signifies truth and the ability to speak directly from the heart. Autumn Equinox takes place during the Celtic tree-month of the Vine. The Celtic letter Muin and the letter M are the letter names for Vine.

Ivy: Hardy, Tenacious Energies

The Ivy is an evergreen vine that can either ramble or climb. Ivy tends to grow in a spiral fashion. It does well under difficult conditions, in poor soil, and in sun or shade. Ivy represents the spiraling search for knowledge within. It is symbolic of succeeding, learning, and growing, even under great difficulty. The Celtic letter Gort and the letter G are the letter names for Ivy.

Reed: The Arrow Reaching Its Mark

The Reed is a very useful plant which grows straight up out of wet land. It resembles the arrow. It was used for musical instruments, combs, fire kindling, and roof thatching. Samhain takes place during the Celtic tree-month of Reed. Winds whistling through the reeds at night can create the sounds of ghosts and of terror, prophetic of the death of the king and of the coming of the death goddess. The Celtic letter Ngetal and the letter N are the letter names for Reed.

Elder: Change, Transition, and Rebirth

The Elder tree has soft, pithy stems. It regenerates itself easily when damaged. It can grow a root from any part of itself. Like the rebirth of the sun, the Elder tree represents return and renewal. It is akin to the cauldron, which is womb and tomb. Elder signifies the end of the old year and the beginning of the new year. The Celtic letter Ruis and the letter R are the letter names for Elder.

SONG OF THE SACRED GROVE

*A powerful group ritual invoking the magic
of the Celtic Trees*

The purpose of this rite is to resolve a societal or political problem; however, it could be adapted for many magical goals. Bringing peace to the people of Earth is the magic done in this example. Thirteen participants will become a coven, and a ring of Sacred Trees, each identifying with one of the Celtic tree-months. (If the rite is done with less than thirteen participants, some will take multiple roles.)

Each Wiccan chooses one (or more if needed) tree to embody. The thirteen powers will blend to become one invincible power, one spiritual flame. There is a statement of magical purpose, a visioning, a working of the Cone of Power, a release of the magic into the Web of Life, and a grounding. This ritual could also be adapted and performed as a magical theater piece.

Preparations for the Rite

ITEMS NEEDED   A cauldron or large stainless steel pot; sand; a second stainless steel or brass bowl (able to hold two cups of liquid) that fits inside the cauldron; three bricks; rubbing alcohol; matches; green leaves with which to surround the cauldron; a censer and censer coal; a small bowl of cedar chips and myrrh; feathers; a red candle; red or yellow flower petals; a cup of water; seashells; a bowl of grain; small stones; a red apple; a broom; a drum; and bread and wine.

THE ALTAR   The altar may be on a table or on the floor. The center of the altar is the cauldron. Create an air space below the cauldron with bricks. Inside the cauldron, place a layer of sand two inches deep. Set the small brass or stainless steel bowl on the sand. Beside the altar have at least two cups of rubbing alcohol and matches. Arrange a ring of green leaves around the cauldron. Set the directions outside the ring of leaves: In the East is a censer and censer coal, a small bowl of myrrh and cedar chips, and feathers arranged around the censer; in the South is a red candle, around which are arranged individual red and yellow flower petals like sun rays; in the West is a chalice of water and seashells; in the North is a bowl of grain, small stones, and a red apple.

TIMING AND INSTRUCTIONS   The duration of this rite is one night, on the full moon. Wear loose, comfortable clothing. Light the censer coal about ten minutes ahead of time. The last thing done is to pour the alcohol into the cauldron. (Test ahead of time how long it takes to burn the alcohol in your cauldron. You will need it to burn for at least twenty to thirty minutes. Be sure you have adequate ventilation in the room.)

Entering the Circle

The Sacred Trees line up in order from Birch to Elder. Birch holds a broom and is at the head. Elder holds a drum and is at the end. A deep slow steady drumbeat begins. The line enters the temple space, while chanting the following (with or without melody). The line circles clockwise around the altar several times, and stops with Birch at the East:

> *A circle are we, a ring of power,*
> *Of Sacred Trees, the Grove in flower.*

Blessing the Circle

With Birch in the East, each participant states his or her presence in the circle by saying his or her tree name in this order:

"Birch is here. Rowan is here. Alder is here. Willow is here. Ash is here. Hawthorn is here. Oak is here. Holly is here. Hazel is here. Vine is here. Ivy is here. Reed is here. Elder is here."

Then Duir steps forward into the circle and says:

> *From Beth, the white dawn*
> *To Ruis, the black cauldron,*
> *We have arisen;*
> *We, who are Danu's children.*
> *I call the Great Mother of Life,*
> *To come and bless this place,*
> *As Birch sweeps the circle clean,*
> *Purifying it with her power.*

All say: *Hail, Danu!*

Birch steps forward with the broom and sweeps the space between the tree ring and the altar, moving in a clockwise direction. As she does so she says repeatedly:

> *Highest power, highest light,*
> *From Anwen descend.*
> *Holy Ones of the Spirit Realm,*
> *Bright blessings send.*

After she has said the above once, the rest may join in with the chant. When done, Birch sets the broom aside.

Calling the Four Quarters

Rowan steps forward into the circle. All begin to hum. Rowan places myrrh and cedar on the censer coal. Standing in the East, arms raised, palms facing out to the East, Rowan says:

> *Spirits of the East,*
> *Of the dawn, and of the crescent Moon,*

> *May these, and all creatures of Air*
> *Bless us.*
> *May Ogmios illuminate our circle with wisdom,*
> *May he guard and guide us,*
> *As we work our magic to aid the world!*

All say: *So be it!*

Rowan moves to the south and faces Alder. Alder raises palms to Rowan. They touch, palm to palm, and Rowan says, *"Air to Fire."*

Alder lights the red candle. The humming continues. Standing in the South, Alder raises arms, palms facing out to the South and says:

> *Spirits of the South,*
> *Of the bright Sun, and the blazing hearth,*
> *May these, the powers of Fire*
> *Bless us.*
> *May Brigid illuminate our circle with passion,*
> *May she guard and guide us,*
> *As we work our magic to aid the world!*

All say: *So be it!*

Alder moves to the West and faces Hawthorn. Hawthorn raises palms to Alder. They touch, palm to palm, and Alder says, *"Fire to Water."*

The humming continues. Standing in the West, Hawthorn raises arms, palms facing out to the West and says:

> *Spirits of the West,*
> *Of deep oceans, and clear flowing streams,*
> *May these, and all creatures of Water*
> *Bless us.*
> *May Coventina fill our circle with joy,*

May she guard and guide us,
As we work our magic to aid the world!

All say: *So be it!*

Hawthorn moves to the North and faces Elder. Elder raises palms to Hawthorn. They touch, palm to palm, and Hawthorn says, *"Water to Earth."*

The humming continues. Standing in the North, Elder raises arms, palms facing out to the North and says:

Spirits of the North,
Of great mountains, and deep rich earth,
May these, and all creatures of Earth
Bless us.
May Cernnunos fill our circle with life and
*   fertile energy,*
May he guard and guide us,
As we work our magic to aid the world!

All say: *So be it!*

Elder goes to Birch and touches hands palm to palm. Elder says:

The circle is cast,
We meet as one.
The circle is cast,
The ritual has begun!

Honoring Mother Earth

Ash steps forward and says:

Now shall we proclaim our love
For our Mother the Earth.
Sacred is Danu's body,

> *Blessed is her flowing bounty,*
> *As is her spirit on high.*
> *We reverence all life on Earth,*
> *And bow our heads in appreciation*
> *For the Great Mother of Life.*
> *All hail, Danu!*

All bow heads and say, "*Hail, Danu!*"

Lighting the Fire

Alder steps forward and says:

> *In the heart resides the spiritual fire.*
> *We have a great purpose here,*
> *To heal the world with peace.*
> *Come, light the fire of your heart*
> *Bring forward your desire,*
> *And we will create change!*

All join hands for a circle dance; moving in a clockwise direction, chant the words below. Try chanting this as a round, adding a second layer of sound by overlapping the first round of lines with the second round of lines:

> *A circle are we, a ring of power,*
> *Of Sacred Trees, the Grove in flower.*

The circle stops and all say, "*We meet to bring peace to Earth.*" Willow steps forward to light the cauldron. First she says:

> *Hail, to Brigid and the Triple Morrigan:*
> *Ana, bring a new dawn unto the hearts of all,*

Macha, bring us your powers of rebirth,
Badba, let the cauldron burn with power!
And Great Brigid bless us all,
As we awaken this Creature of Fire!

Willow sets a lit match into the cauldron. Reaching upward she says:

Mother of the Full Moon,
I draw down your perfect light,
All do the same.
Come draw her down,
To enchant the flaming cauldron.
Now all, draw her power down.

All reach upward and with the breath, draw her power down.

Willow throws cedar and myrrh into the fire, saying:

Cauldron, cedar, myrrh, and Moon
Bright desire enchanted fire.
Cauldron, cedar, myrrh and Moon,

Silver bright, Full Moon light,
Cauldron, cedar, myrrh, and Moon,
Magic rise on Sabbat Night!

Again Willow guides all to draw the full moon power down through raised hands, and together send it into the flame through the palms of the hands while chanting:

MA (MMM-Ahh. . . .)

Willow says: *Moon has entered fire.*
           The cauldron is prepared.

Song of the Sacred Grove

Hawthorn steps forward. Hawthorn will now call for each Wiccan to become the power of their tree, for their power to become pure, selfless, and of the highest spirit. Hawthorn says:

> *Come, brothers and sisters . . .*
> *Birch, Rowan, Alder, Willow, Ash,*
> *Hawthorn, Oak, Holly, and Hazel,*
> *Vine, Ivy, Reed, and Elder.*
> *Let the Song of the Grove*
> *Be heard!*

Here, each Tree, beginning with Birch, states their poetic affirmation, one after the other in a clockwise direction.

Birch: *I am the light of every dawn.*
Rowan: *I am the magic between the worlds.*
Alder: *I am the fire in darkest night.*
Willow: *I am the magic of the changing moon.*
Ash: *I am the union of Earth and Sky.*
Hawthorn: *I am the purity of the white Mayblossom.*
Oak: *I am the door to every hope.*
Holly: *I am the battle won without blood.*
Hazel: *I am the key to the waters of life.*
Vine: *I am the wisdom of unsung truth.*
Ivy: *I am the spiral of whirling time.*
Reed: *I am the arrow that finds its mark.*
Elder: *I am the cauldron, empty yet full.*

Elder begins a slow steady beat of the drum. Oak says:

> *Brothers and sisters,*
> *Through the power of Duir*
> *We shall enter the door*
> *Unto the Holy Realms.*

Where we become as one.
Together, pure spirit will
Enter the door of power.
We shall be one . . .
One circle, one power.

All say: *One circle, one power.*

Holly says:

The peace of Earth is our goal.
To success we shall ascend.

Power of the Sacred Grove

Hazel says:

Sacred Grove, join hands
And turn thy attention
Unto the blessed Earth.
See our world, its blue seas,
Green forests, and great mountains,
See our world teeming with life.
The world awaits our blessing.

All say: *And so it shall be.*

Vine speaks:

May those whose hearts are dark
Now feel the light of love.
Love enters into shadow.
Compassion shall arise in every heart.
With our strength,
Will understanding grow between the races,
As the people of Earth turn toward peace.

All say: *And so it shall be.*

Ivy speaks:

> *May the spiral of life*
> *Move toward peace,*
> *Taking with it the hearts of all.*
> *Taking all unto kinder and gentler ways,*
> *To even the darkest heart,*
> *Is this promise given.*

All say: *And so it shall be.*

Reed speaks:

> *In the heart of the grove has peace arisen.*
> *And kindness and shining compassion.*
> *Noble is the understanding that all are not*
>   *perfect.*
> *And so we forgive ourselves, and others*
> *And bring all together*
> *Unto the light of fair Brigid.*
> *See, believe, know,*
> *And the magic shall be done,*
> *Just as the arrow finds its true mark.*

All say: *And so it shall be.*

Fire of Rebirth

Elder speaks:

> *To heal and save the blessed Earth.*
> *The cauldron has become the Womb of Rebirth.*
> *To the center, your powers send,*
> *Our separate gifts, one power blend.*

Fire Dance

All join hands. Chant the following while circling around the fire:

> *Luna's power, bright moon hour,*
> *Fire to bless us and. . . . . magic flow!*

Over this, Hazel says:

> *Sacred Grove, look upon the fire.*
> *See a column of energy spiraling upward from it.*
> *Come, add the words which are your gifts.*
> *Add them to the rising spiral above the flame.*
> *Speak out, come Elder, begin . . .*

One by one the Sacred Trees call out the gifts of their powers. Each draws up the power of Earth, through their roots. Then each speaks the words of blessing carefully, visioning that they send them into the center of the circle, to the column of spiraling energy above the fire.

Visioning Magic

In a group visualization, Reed guides all to draw energy again up through their roots, and down from the skies, sending their powers to the flame. It grows into a shining sphere of spiritual light and joins with the flame. Reed charges that forgiveness, empathy, and understanding, enter the hearts of all who live. And so love grows in the heart of the Grove, and enters the holy fire.

Into the Web of Life

Oak speaks:

> *Now shall we send our holy fire,*
> *Which is our prayer for peace into the world.*
> *See the Web of life, connecting all things to*
>   *each other.*
> *Its strands hang gently in the air,*
> *Glistening . . . shining . . .*
> *The Web is everywhere,*
> *And one strand leads to all the others*
> *And so it is, around the world.*
> *All things live within the Web.*
>
> *Our magic is alive, its energy just above the*
>   *sacred cauldron.*
> *And so we shall bind the spell, and release it*
>   *into the Web of Life.*

Holly repeats the words of peace, and seals them. She says:

> *First, I lay the words upon this spell,*
> *That peace may come to Earth.*
> *Wherein the magic goes, it shall be so,*
> *Its end result to bring the gifts of peace.*
> *And so I seal this spell.*

Binding and Grounding

Willow calls for the Binding Chant. All join hands. The chant is repeated nine times, building energy as it goes. All chant:

> *And now by the power of three times three,*
> *As we will it, so shall it be!*

Ivy leads the Grounding. At the final, *so shall it be!* of the Binding chant, Ivy directs the trees to let go their power and release it into the Web, and to fall forward at the waist, or to the ground, as they release. Ivy guides the deep breath and release, to make each mind quiet and still.

Bread and Wine

After the Grounding, Hawthorn offers the bread and Vine offers the wine, saying *"May you never hunger,"* at the giving of bread, and *"May you never thirst"* at the giving of wine.

Closing the Circle

Those who invoked the four directions now thank and release them, going in a counterclockwise direction, from Elder to Hawthorn to Alder to Rowan.

Rowan closes the circle and bids the "Merry part" farewell:

> *Sacred Grove, our work is done,*
> *Our magic sent 'round the world,*
> *So merry meet, and merry part,*
> *And merry meet again!*

Bibliography

Blair, Peter. *Roman Britain and Early England*. Edinburgh: Thomas Nelson and Sons Ltd., 1963.

Bogdanovich, Peter. *A Year and a Day Engagement Calendar*. Woodstock, N.Y.: Overlook Press, 1991.

Buckland, Raymond. *The Tree: The Complete Book of Saxon Witchcraft*. New York: Samuel Weiser, 1974.

Cavendish, Richard, ed. *Mythology: An Illustrated Encyclopedia*. New York: Rizzoli International Publications, 1980.

Eisler, Riane. *The Chalice and the Blade*. San Francisco: Harper and Row, 1987.

Eliade, Mircea. *Rites and Symbols of Initiation*. New York: Harper and Row, 1975.

Farrar, Janet and Stewart. *Eight Sabbats for Witches*. London: Robert Hale Ltd., 1985.

Flaum, Eric. *Encyclopedia of Mythology: Gods, Heroes, Legends*. Philadelphia: Courage, 1993.

Gardner, Gerald. *Witchcraft Today*. London: Rider Publications, 1954.

Gardner, Gerald, *The Meaning of Witchcraft*. London: Aquarian Press, 1959.

Garmonsway, G. N., trans. *The Anglo-Saxon Chronicle*. New York: E.P. Dutton, 1953.

Grant, Michael. *Gods and Mortals in Classical Mythology*. Springfield, Mass.: G. & C. Merriam, 1972.

Graves, Robert. *Greek Myths; Vol. I & II*. London: Penguin Books, 1984.

Graves, Robert. *The White Goddess*. London: Octagon Books, 1972.

Getty, Adele. *Goddess: Mother of Living Nature*. London: Thames and Hudson, 1990.

Harner, Michael. *The Way of the Shaman*. New York: Bantam Books, 1982.

Leek, Sybil. *Diary of a Witch*. New York: Signet, 1968.

Leek, Sybil. *The Complete Art of Witchcraft*. New York: Signet, 1971.

Mercatante, Anthony. *Encyclopedia of World Mythology and Legend*. New York: Facts on File, 1988.

Murray, Liz and Colin. *The Celtic Tree Oracle*. New York: St. Martin's Press, 1988.

Murray, Margaret. *The Witch Cult in Western Europe*. London: Oxford University Press, 1921.

Murray, Margaret. *The God of the Witches*. Essex: Daimon Press, 1931.

Roman Catholic Church, The. *The New Catholic Encyclopedia; Vol. VI, VII, and X*. New York: McGraw Hill, 1967.

Saklatvala, Beram. *The Origins of the English People*. New York: Taplinger Publishing, 1970.

Starhawk. *The Spiral Dance*. San Francisco: Harper Collins, 1979.

Stevens, Joseph and Lena. *Secrets of Shamanism*. New York: Avon Books, 1988.

Stone, Merlin. *When God Was a Woman*. New York: Harvest Books, 1978.

Van De Weyer, ed. *Celtic Fire*. New York: Bantam Doubleday Dell, 1990.

Walker, Barbara. *The Women's Encyclopedia of Myths and Secrets*. San Francisco: Harper and Row, 1983.

Williamson, Robin. *The Wise and Foolish Tongue*. San Francisco: Chronicle Books, 1991.

About the Author

JENNIFER REIF, artist, poet, and musician, has studied the relationships between nature, ancient cultures, and their mythologies since 1983. She taught classes on Wicca and Goddess Religion in the Los Angeles area for many years, through Memosyne Arts and Studies, Long Beach Woman-Spirit, the Pallas Society, and Circle of Aradia. In 1992 she released *Mysteries of Earth*, an album of original Goddess-Pagan songs, distributed by Serpentine Music. Her first book, *Mysteries of Demeter: Rebirth of the Pagan Way*, was published in 1999. Jennifer loves late Victorian Art, computers that work, gardening, a good cup of coffee, lavender nail polish, and cats. She lives in Venice, California. Visit her Web site at www.demeter.spiritualitea.net.